SIGN UP & SAVE

Grand Street—straight from the jagged edge of the imagination. Fiction, Art, Poetry, Science. Travel, Photography. Expect the unexpected

D0851589

S...

Name_____
(Please Print)

Address_____

City_____

State_____ Zip_____

GRAND STREET

☐ O... ...ear (4 issues)   **$24**
Save $10 off the cover price.

☐ **Two Years** (8 issues)   **$42**
Save $26 off the cover price.

☐ Renewal   ☐ Payment enclosed
☐ New order   ☐ Bill me

Please add $10 for all foreign and Canadian orders.
Payable in U.S. funds only.

2242A

SEND GIFTS & SAVE

First Gift or New Subscription:
One Year (4 issues)   **$24**

Additional Gifts:
One Year (4 issues)   only **$21**

My Name_____
(Please Print)
Address_____

City_____

State_____ Zip_____

☐ Renewal   ☐ Payment enclosed
☐ New order   ☐ Bill me

Please add $10 for all foreign and Canadian orders.
Payable in U.S. funds only.

GRAND STREET

Gift Subscription(s) to:

Name_____
(Please Print)

Address_____

City_____

State_____ Zip_____

Name_____
(Please Print)

Address_____

City_____

State_____ Zip_____

A gift card will be sent in your name.

2242B

BUSINESS REPLY MAIL

FIRST CLASS   PERMIT NO. 301   DENVILLE, NJ

POSTAGE WILL BE PAID BY ADDRESSEE

GRAND STREET

Subscription Services, Dept. GRS
P.O. Box 3000
Denville, NJ 07834-9878

BUSINESS REPLY MAIL

FIRST CLASS   PERMIT NO. 301   DENVILLE, NJ

POSTAGE WILL BE PAID BY ADDRESSEE

GRAND STREET

Subscription Services, Dept. GRS
P.O. Box 3000
Denville, NJ 07834-9878

Editor
Clayton Eshleman

Contributing Editors
Rachel Blau DuPlessis
Michael Palmer
Eliot Weinberger

Correspondents
Charles Bernstein
James Clifford
Clark Coolidge
Marjorie Perloff
Jerome Rothenberg
Jed Rasula
Marjorie Welish

Managing Editor
Caryl Eshleman

Editorial Assistant
L. Kay Miller

Sulfur is Antaeus with a risk. It has efficacy. It has primacy. It is one of the few magazines that is more than a receptacle of talent, actually contributing to the shape of present day literary engagement.
— George Butterick

Sulfur must certainly be the most important literary magazine which has explored and extended the boundaries of poetry. Eshleman has a nose for smelling out what is going to happen next in the ceaseless evolution of the living art.
— James Laughlin

In an era of literary conservatism and sectarianism, the broad commitment of *Sulfur* to both literary excellence and a broad interdisciplinary, unbought humanistic engagement with the art of poetry has been invaluable. Its critical articles have been the sharpest going over the last several years.
— Gary Snyder

Founded at the California Institute of Technology in 1981, Sulfur magazine is now based at Eastern Michigan University. Funded by the National Endowment for the Arts since 1983, and winner of four General Electric Foundation Awards for Younger Writers, it is an international magazine of poetry and poetics, archetypal psychology, paleolithic imagination, artwork and art criticism, translations and archival materials. Some of our featured contributors have been: Artaud, Pound, Golub, Vallejo, Olson, Niedecker, Riding, Césaire, Kitaj, and Hillman. We appear twice a year (April and November) in issues of 250 pages. Current subscription rates: $13 for 2 issues for individuals ($19 for institutions). Single copies are $8.00. Numbers 1, 15, 17 and 19 are only available in complete sets (1-27) at $235.00.

GRAND STREET

42

Cover: Sherrie Levine, *Untitled (After Duchamp: Chessboards) #4* (detail), 1989.

Grand Street is set in ITC New Baskerville by Crystal Graphics, Houston, Tex., and printed by W. E. Barnett & Associates, Houston, Tex. Color separations and halftones are by Color Separations, Inc., Houston, Tex.

Grand Street (ISSN 0734-5496; ISBN 0-393-30858-8) is published quarterly by Grand Street Press (a project of the New York Foundation for the Arts, Inc., a not-for-profit corporation), 131 Varick Street, #906, New York, N.Y. 10013. Contributions and gifts to Grand Street Press, a project of the New York Foundation for the Arts, Inc., are tax-deductible to the extent allowed by law.

Unsolicited material should be addressed to the editors at *Grand Street,* 131 Varick Street, #906, New York, N.Y. 10013. Manuscripts will not be returned unless accompanied by a stamped, self-addressed envelope.

Second-class postage at New York, N.Y., and additional mailing offices. Postmaster: Please send address changes to Subscription Service, Dept. GRS, P.O. Box 3000, Denville, N.J. 07834.

Subscription orders and address changes should be addressed to Subscription Service, Dept. GRS, P.O. Box 3000, Denville, N.J. 07834. Subscriptions are $24 a year (four issues). Foreign subscriptions (including Canada) are $34 a year, and must be payable in U.S. funds. Single-copy price is $8.50. *Grand Street* is distributed to the trade by W. W. Norton & Company, 500 Fifth Avenue, New York, N.Y. 10110, and to newsstands only by B. DeBoer, Inc., 113 E. Centre St., Nutley, N.J. 07110.

GRAND STREET

Editor

Jean Stein

Managing Editor

Brooke Allen

Poetry Editor

Erik Rieselbach

Assistant Editors

Sarah Chace

Paige Crowley

Howard Halle

Intern

Anthony Perliss

Art Editor

Walter Hopps

Designer

Don Quaintance

Production Assistant

Elizabeth Frizzell

Copy Editor

Kate Norment

Contributing Editors

Morgan Entrekin, Raymond Foye, Jonathan Galassi,
Andrew Kopkind, Alberto Manguel, Edward W. Said,
Robert Scheer, Jean Strouse, Jeremy Treglown,
Katrina vanden Heuvel, Shelley Wanger, Drenka Willen

Publishers

Jean Stein & Torsten Wiesel

CONTENTS

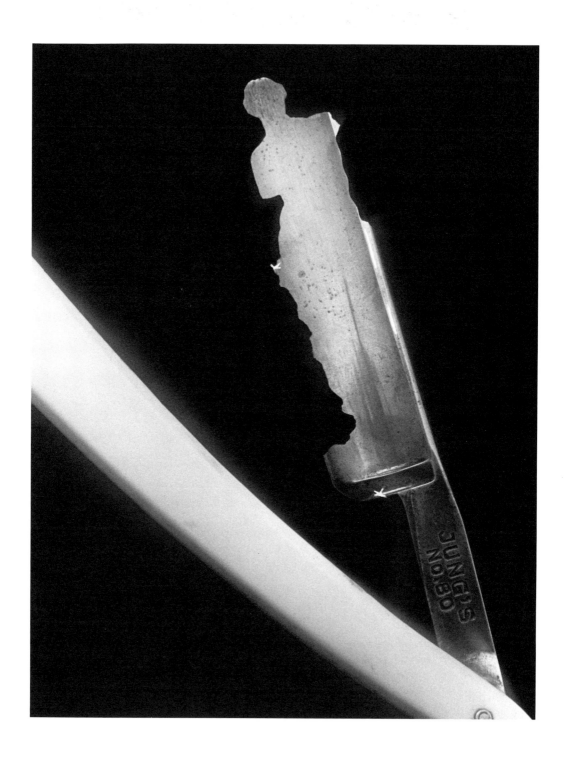

The Passenger

I didn't notice she was dead until the second or third month, maybe even later; I can't recall exactly. It seems ridiculous now, how slow I was to catch on, yet there's no way I can deceive myself: it took three or four months, forty to sixty trips, maybe more, to convince me she was dead. And the amazing thing is that the discovery didn't come as a shock to me at all. I just said to myself, as if it were an obvious fact: "So that's it: she's dead." And everything went on just as before.

Of course, it's easier to understand my lack of surprise, the fact that I didn't scream or try to jump off the number 17 bus, my bus, when you consider that until that moment nothing unusual had ever happened to me. I'm an ordinary man, I live an ordinary life, I have an ordinary job, an ordinary wife, an ordinary home. . . . I'm not accustomed to unusual things, so I don't know how people react to them. I received that information, or gift, or message from beyond the grave, with perfect calm. "Of course! She's dead," I thought.

Before I arrived at that conclusion, what had called my attention to this passenger was that she didn't resemble my wife at all. There she was, in her seat, sitting up straight, expressionless, her eyes blank, her cheeks a rosy color that accentuated the bright pallor of her skin. My wife is much more nervous, she's always in motion, with jerky movements, darting eyes that never stop searching from place to place, as if she had always just mislaid her purse.

I think that I first became obsessed with the passenger in the belief that she would relieve the monotony of my trips, which were always the same, although I didn't find their inert sameness unpleasant. I didn't read the newspaper. Until then I had looked out the window of the number 17 bus, quietly scrutinizing minute changes: a larger crowd at the Tibidabo bakery; the new spot where the city sweeper, a dirty man in a carrot-colored uniform, was working, up or down the tangle of Balmes Street; the schoolchildren dashing between the buses with an agility so upsetting it makes you wish they'd get hit. But that's outrageous. We don't have children. Perhaps that's why my wife is always panting, as if she had lost something. And then she's very emotional. She cries a lot. And that tears me apart. Because she is innocent.

The passenger made a welcome change. Very different from the other women who ride the number 17 with me, pathetic middle-aged women, carrying useless bundles and useless sorrows. Hardly any men ride the bus; they all have cars, in which they enclose themselves and drive aimlessly from place to place, just to be alone for a while, so they don't go crazy. Their women, the ones on the bus, laugh only when they see other women as totally broken-down as themselves. Creation has fallen apart completely, that's what I see in this. Nothing else matters to me, that's the reason I don't read newspapers: world hunger, democracy in Latin America, pollution, apartheid in South Africa . . . trivia. It's these women who want to die but endure until they finally collapse, that's what moves me.

But not the passenger, no. Now I can laugh at how ingenuous I was, but when I first noticed her, I thought: "At last, a woman who doesn't wish she were dead." Of course not; she was dead. But I didn't know that then. I stared at her, with her distant and indifferent look, her hair carefully coiled, her hands resting quietly on her knees, and I admired her, I admired her internal life, the harmony that was so obvious. What a contrast to my wife, always in despair, the pressure of life always weighing on her foundering body, a body that was never beautiful but is now so worn by time as to seem scarcely human. She's modest, my wife, and she hides in the bathroom to change her clothes. She feels a deep shame, like all people who have been injured by time. I try to avoid her, but I have occasionally run into her, by chance, when she's engaged in one of her innumerable obsessive hygienic rituals, and I couldn't avoid seeing her belly, or her buttocks, or her breasts, or her thighs. My god! What a horror! I hide my reaction. I avert my eyes. But it's no use, she knows that I've seen her and she blushes like a schoolgirl. As soon as she's alone, she weeps. She stares into the mirror, her hand at her throat, and she weeps.

And what makes me think this woman doesn't wish she were dead? First of all, she always chooses the seat right behind the bus driver, the seat that (to put it dramatically) faces the crowd with defiance. I can't say that I have ever actually seen her make this choice. To tell the truth, when I got on the bus, she was always already sitting in the front seat. Now I'm going to skip to something I should really leave till later. On the fourth or fifth trip, I started to go up Balmes Street, to different bus stops, trying to find out where the passenger got on, but no matter how far I went, I never managed to get on before her. After a month, when I had completed the circuit of stops (the ones on Republica Argentina, the ones on Rambla de Cataluña, the ones on Via Layetana) without success, since I always found her in her seat when I got on, the fact that she was dead began to dawn on me as a possible explanation.

She seemed to take no notice of anything or anyone, she wasn't interested in anything or anyone. That was the second thing that made me think she didn't wish she were dead. People who can barely tolerate their existence are constantly looking around for distractions. I'm the same, distracting myself with the bakery, the street sweeper, the children. And so are my companions on these trips, gaping at billboards on which men and women, cars and buildings all are laid bare. Or more likely, bitterly studying hands, the rings on those hands; feet, the shoes on those feet; heads, the hair on those heads. Continually moving on to smaller and smaller things, searching for signs and signals that the end is near, the termination of a sorrow that can't be concealed.

Not her. Nothing and no one engaged her attention. Impassive, at peace with herself and the universe, perhaps borne along by a lofty thought or a holy memory, some way to live, some way to make survival a luxury and an art. That is what attracted me to her. Until she looked at me. It was inevitable. I knew it from the first day.

I have already set down one item regarding my growing conviction that she was dead. Now I'm going to give another. It must have been sometime in the second or third month—as if I could remember, in my present state!—when we had sat facing each other for quite a while, she in the front seat, I in one of the middle ones, always on the aisle. I will never forget it, although its importance has now diminished for me. Her most unusual feature was her reddish cheeks, inflamed by nature, some quirk of coloring, since her face bore not the least trace of cosmetics or makeup, and it was those red slashes that made my blood freeze. Because their tone deepened. I had to be sure, as if to awaken from a dream. I looked more closely, and there could be no doubt: the red slashes had suddenly darkened.

I know it's hard to believe, but contemplating those cheeks unsettled me so thoroughly that I didn't grasp the reason for their darkening, despite the fact that it was perfectly simple: the red slashes got darker by becoming more concentrated as they diminished in size. And the reason they had diminished in size was that the passenger was smiling. She was smiling at me. And when I shifted my eyes to expand my field of vision to take in her whole face, I felt a sharp prickle along my spine, and my mind went blank. The dead woman was looking at me and smiling. At me!

Of course, it's true that it wasn't a living smile; it wasn't the smile of those women who try to force themselves upon the attention of the bus driver when buying a ticket or the ticket taker when showing a pass for him to examine or collect; smiles arising from a doglike humility, from an insatiable hunger to be part of the world and mean something to someone; smiles that cover a willingness to surrender themselves completely, their broken-down and useless bodies, to the first stranger ready to pay them a moment's notice. The dead woman did not smile like that. Her smile was infinitely discreet: she gave off no more than the hint of a smile, it barely curled the corners of her mouth, it barely lifted her cheeks, but it darkened the spots on her cheekbones.

In fact, she didn't have to move a muscle, because really it was her eyes that were smiling, and not by arching her eyebrows or by creating a cluster of wrinkles in the corners. Her eyes remained still, metallic, but they smiled, and they were locked with mine.

I had to rest both hands on the seat and turn my eyes toward the window (then to the window on the other side, on my right) to keep myself from falling, struck by vertigo. The woman who was sharing my seat made a sudden movement, as if she'd been asleep and had awakened terrified at seeing a passenger she didn't recognize. She thrashed nervously for a while, mumbling words I couldn't catch, before calming down when she realized she hadn't missed her stop. Then I could return to the passenger, but she was no longer looking at me. Once again she was as remote as a totem.

This was something extraordinary, something unusual, and it was happening to me. How could I stay calm? I'm not a person who can deal with events that require superhuman and heroic courage, as well as great cleverness, and quick reflexes, and per-haps warmth and wisdom, I don't know. I don't know what virtues they possess, the people who experience unusual things, messages or messengers from the most distant powers . . . or the closest ones. The closest powers, but hard to reach. Men much abler and worthier than I, with greater faculties of understanding, with open and generous minds, have spent their lives studying, praying that something like this would happen to them, and their prayers have gone unanswered. And against all expectations, it was I, the lowliest, the least gifted one, who received such a sign from out of the darkness, from the infinite distance that is nonetheless so close. After this sublime exchange of glances, I resolved to be wor-thy of this sign, this message. Lowly as I was, I resolved to accom-plish what was sure to be demanded of me.

The most painful part was not that I had to keep myself in check at home, with my wife. Our habits were set in stone, draped in a nice automatism that allowed me to perform my everyday acts with my head in another world, in the world to which I now belonged. I ate supper with her and accepted the looks she gave me, looks charged with complaint. I sat next to her, in front of the television; as always, I held her right hand, which was small and fleshy; she leaned her head on my shoulder, as always; and then I lost myself in ecstasy, rapture. The chosen people don't change—they shouldn't change—even the smallest detail of their lives. They have to take refuge behind an impenetrable facade.

I never lost sleep, nor did I find myself besieged by bad dreams. Just the opposite: as soon as I removed my dressing gown and slippers, as soon as I gave my wife the same kiss I gave her every night, I slept peacefully, never stirring, all night long. On the other hand, I noticed a slight change in the mornings. Now I awoke instantly, with no fatigue, my head clear and ready for action, just the way, as a child, I read that Tarzan, king of the apes, would awaken.

No, no, it wasn't my home life that was painful, nor the bureaucratic routine in my office at the hydroelectric company. What was painful was the exchange of signals that took place between us on the number 17 bus. What was painful was discharging the obligations of a chosen man in a universe of pain and doubt. The will that I had never needed, that I had never exerted in school, or in business college, or during the hard months of military service, now became essential to me; and the constant exercise of self-control and self-concealment, to hide the power and exhilaration that had possessed me, left me completely out of breath.

From the day of our mutual recognition, I put myself entirely at the disposal of the dead woman and those who had sent her to me. By tiny signals, invisible to the other passengers, I let her know that I was entirely at her service and that I would like to know as soon as possible what actions were expected of me. I raised my eyebrows almost imperceptibly, still holding her gaze like a magnet. Then I raised them a little more, very quickly, asking her what was required of me. She tilted her head slightly, indicating that such haste was inappropriate. But I insisted, opening my mouth a bit, like a tiny yawn, to make my request a little stronger. She ducked her head briefly, reproaching me for my vehemence. Day after day, this went on. Wonderful days!

There was only one occasion when I almost lost control. I should confess that it was partially premeditated, and so, no doubt, to some extent done with her knowledge. The evening before, my good wife had taken ill, and as a result of her nervous condition she suffered a dizzy spell and fell into a faint, dragging the tablecloth with her, as well as all the dishes: the soup bowl, two plates, a bottle of mineral water, the usual things, in short. I went to her aid, but found her in a highly excited state. She was striking her fists against the floor and screaming (not very loud, because of the neighbors) that she couldn't go on, she was too miserable. I consoled her as best I could, and as I put my arms around this mass of tortured flesh, I felt a great sorrow. I took her to her room, where she collapsed like a sick horse. "What has become of me! What do I have left?" she wailed, calming down slowly, by degrees; but before falling asleep, she had another nervous outburst and pulled at a tuft of hair on the left side of her head, showing it to me the way you would an ulcerated leg or an abscess. "Do you understand? You at least can see!" she moaned. Soon she slumped over asleep, next to me, and that was when I formulated my plan.

The next day I sent the usual signals to the passenger, but I saw immediately that she was aware of my intentions. She didn't return the customary signals, rather she revealed a new one: a tiny frown wrinkling the skin between her eyebrows. I didn't weaken, but began to chant inside me: "I must do it, I must do it." Her frown grew more menacing and evil. We got to my stop, and I clung to my seat, as I had made up my mind to do, and let it go past. As I did so, her forehead underwent a convulsion such as only I could appreciate, so that it resembled a bird, with a life of its own, that could fly at my face and tear my eyes from their sockets. I sprang to my feet, terrified, and got off at the next stop. My plan had been thwarted. I had been sharply prevented from varying my habits in the slightest. But the powers had been informed of my growing impatience. That was my one and only rebellion.

I still could not take the initiative. I waited patiently for that most hidden and most manifest power to do as it pleased with me. I continued holding "conversations" but repressed my urge to act, my urge to prove I was worthy of the sign and the message. It's true that I did intensify my questioning, trying to find out if I was called on to save her, to intercede for her; if she (or perhaps others) expected me to intervene for her in some mysterious way that would redound to her benefit, that would bring her relief if relief was what she needed, redemption if she was awaiting redemption. The microscopic horizontal trembling of her jawbone, which hit me like a roar of laughter, a roar that was deafening but, astonishingly, soundless, convinced me that my intercession had not been planned for the benefit of the passenger.

No. Even now, there's no room for doubt. If I hadn't been such a run-of-the-mill person, such a washed-out character, if I had not had such limited experience of life, I would have found the situation intolerable. Every day, every hour, I told myself that this was exactly what they wanted from me: patience, high resolve, stoicism, self-control, disdain for the baser passions and stirrings of the heart. As if little by little they were turning me into a copy of the passenger, her duplicate, though formed of a lower material. And only when I had attained her cool self-possession would I be fit to act, could I move on to intervene in some way. I repeated that thought to myself day after day, hour after hour. I could only tolerate it (so I profoundly believe, now that no alternative remains) thanks to being so very insignificant myself, thanks to being surrounded by people infinitely stronger than I, more substantial, more used to occupying a space on this (very narrow) earth, as if they deserved to do so.

And my hour arrived unexpectedly, without warning, just as the hour I had been chosen had. I noticed nothing unusual on that terrible morning. I said good-bye to my wife, stroking the hand with which she was trying, as usual, to conceal the folds of her neck. The street was boiling with people bustling to schools and businesses: children piling into vans, mothers wearing gloomy faces, unfriendly shopkeepers, crooked policemen. Also police and ambulance sirens, newspapers flying around everywhere as if they'd come to life, dogs with cold noses and spoiled eyes. The sun, the same. The sky, as always. I could add (but this is something I can see now, not something I felt then) that my head felt lighter than usual and that the noise of the city seemed louder and struck me more forcibly. I got onto the number 17, walked by the passenger . . . and the proof began to arrive. Until that day, when I walked past her, trying not to look at her, I had never touched her. But this time I felt her hand slide across mine, in passing, like a fish brushing against a swimmer almost imperceptibly. There was a sudden chill; it came over me suddenly and still has not left me. It still has not left me.

With my jaw clenched I moved toward the middle of the bus looking for a seat, but there weren't any. I went back to the front. There was a space, like the open door of the tomb of Christ, the seat facing the passenger. Never before had I been able to look at her up close. Now, trembling with fear and cold, trying to keep my teeth from chattering, I was but a few feet from her. Her eyes fastened on me like leeches, and I lost all sense of time, of what was happening around me. Her eyes sucked out all that was left of me, the way prehistoric warriors sucked the bones of their enemies. I was left empty, hollow, as light as a sheet of paper. A husk suspended at the mercy of a gust of air from the other world.

I don't know how much time passed. I have lost all memory of those moments, of those hours in which I lived in the will of the dead, dangling above an unruffled abyss of nothingness. I saw the passenger rise up like the flame that guided the Ark of Israel. It grew taller than a camel and blew through the bus in a swirl of air that formed a space around it. Thus I followed her on her fiery path, like a will-o'-the-wisp blown by the wind. I could barely make out what was passing before my eyes: clouds that formed and then vanished, odd discharges of light and sound that exploded into flowers of dust; I felt fine scratches against my face as if I were breaking through hot, dry spiderwebs, and, finally, a perfect circle of glass and the dead woman in the center, an object glowing in her hand.

The door of my house stood in front of me; I recognized it without any difficulty as the day slipped back toward normal. It was safe and familiar and made warm gases start to expand inside me, and I looked down at the ends of my arms and saw my hands. Now I knew what it was that death was rattling: it was my key and we were going to enter my house because my intercession was going to take place there, in my home. A grateful prayer rose to my throat and my joy was so great that I tore at my garments.

The dead woman was in the living room, in an unlikely place: she was standing behind the chair where my wife was sitting, hands in her lap, looking up at me expectantly. My wife's features had been transformed; they were illuminated with the ethereal calm of an Italian painting. Without any effort at all, I saw her then as she had been many years before: her radiant infancy, her glorious youth, her ripe maturity, and all the love that she had felt until that moment. Until that final moment. And her former voice, fresh and fine, with more coloration; she greeted me joyfully, with the spontaneous need of people who can't be separated. Now we were reunited by the fullness of our passion and the life-giving liquid of our conjoinings, the light that must sometimes illuminate our lives, the lives of all mortals, all those condemned to appear and then vanish, to blaze and be extinguished.

But the key to my house, the key to my home life and to the mystery of usury, expense, and consumption, sparkled in the hand of death, changed into a razor to whose virile silvery light I had to surrender. Now death was a colossus covered in white rags, crowned with a yellow bone that shone with the gleam of metal. I didn't draw back, because until then I had been held in the grip of a force stronger than both of us, stronger even than the passenger. I was to be an instrument of vengeance against Father Time, against the stupidity of Father Time and its cruelty. I didn't draw back, because my wife was raising her arms and begging for my embrace, the embrace that would strengthen her against all harm and against the violence of those greater than us, the embrace that would form a new, more vigorous being, a moist and fertile trunk.

But even so, it wasn't me. I swear that I was going to do it and I could have done it, but I didn't do it. Kindness and love pushed me toward the razor and toward the neck that was not protected by her hand anymore, but I didn't manage to do it. It wasn't exactly an angel who stepped between the knife and the neck of the victim. It was she, the passenger, who turned with an impeccable classical move, with the grace and balance of a reaper, and cut the neck of my wife and let the ancient blood flow.

To those who accuse me now, to those who look at me condemningly, I can make no reply. To those who seized me, I could make no reply. In my soul I hold fast to the honor of having been chosen, and to my innocence, my hands unstained by that fatal compassion I felt. I have been a witness to vengeance, and I know that there are powers close to us though far away. Now, some tremble in fear, others rejoice. But the powers will change, and those who rejoice will later be shaken. And this will go on forever and ever. Until the end of our father, Time.

Translated by Carol Christensen and Thomas Christensen

Ripples on the Surface

"Ripples on the surface of the water
were silver salmon passing under—different
from the sorts of ripples caused by breezes"

A scudding plume on the wave—
a humpback whale is
breaking out in air up
gulping herring
  —Nature not a book, but a *performance*, a
high old culture

Ever-fresh events
scraped out, rubbed out, and used, used, again—
the braided channels of the rivers
hidden under fields of grass—

The vast wild.
  the house, alone.
the little house in the wild,
  the wild in the house.

both forgotten.

    No nature.

Both together, one big empty house.

Mood

I

She walks down Oxford Street.

When she heard that high, loud, educated voice she saw the Blue
Train where it was so much in evidence, then the boat where
was no sound of it throughout the crossing, the English Pullman
where again it triumphed, crying: My dear I went to sleep before
the boat started and didn't wake up till my maid told me we were
in. My dear, that same voice said, what people want is to lie naked
in the sun and that drives everyone further south to where it's
all unknown. There was that same kind of voice, here in Oxford
Street, this time proclaiming: The most lovely sponge. She looked
and there was that same kind of woman coming out of a shop.
—A most lovely sponge which—and then several buses cut short its
price and the story of how that sponge was bought. She wondered
where that woman bought her sponges. One shouldn't go just
anywhere for one's sponge. For what is a sponge—and this she
felt but did not think. Why it is picked from the sea, it is cleaned
and dried, perhaps a lot of things are done to it, perhaps nothing
very much. Perhaps a little salt is still left in it. Here she sailed. For,
when she heard that woman talk, so she remembered the clatter
of knives and forks, the absolute roar of chassis and good living
and she remembered how, in the Pullman, she had longed to be
in a restaurant again where it was famous and lots of people you

knew. She said no I will never go abroad again, unless I go with a thousand people, it's really too squalid there being just three or four of you. The sea and everything, it just won't do, she said, if there isn't a whole crowd one knows. It's like going when you're by yourself and turning on the gramophone. Or like a sponge in the water in an empty bath.

Where did that woman buy her sponges? When you saw her kind get into the Pullman with just the right sort of shabbiness in their clothes, then you thought of her lying in the sun, clean, clean, clean to the last little bit. Why had she herself never considered sponges? It was because you didn't have to buy them often that you were rather haphazard about it. Everything else had the right shops and places but she'd never heard of there being one place for these. She looked at the stockings in the window. She accused herself. It was squalid, dirty in her not to have been more careful about her sponges. Absolutely filthy really.

That was what older women did to you, they made you feel rather squalid. Except when you went in bathing dresses, the blue sea and you and they being cadaverous on the sand. Even in the hotel afterwards when you were all dressed up and when they could afford to be so much better dressed than you was still the echo of the sea and your bathing dress round you, like it might be you had nothing on at all. So merely from being young, and your body being more or less naturally thin and not just skinny, you felt you were better than all the older ones in the place you were. Till you got into the train and there were hundreds with those voices. You hadn't seen them on their beaches nor had their men seen you coming out of the sea. And at once their experience put you at a disadvantage, made you feel dirty.

As a botanist knows the best place for his flowers and he will set out and go straight to where he has found that sort before, where he will find them again, under that bank or by those stones on the hill, so they knew so much more about shops. If a man was fond of flowers as a boy and grew up in that fondness, so as the years went by he would learn more and more where he would be likely to find some particular flower, on a slope looking east or out looking west, and also what combination of shade or wet was most favorable to its growth. As he grew older so he would know more and more, and it wouldn't be just book learning. So, because they had been so much longer at it, older people knew better where to look for things. And as an older man might be most careful where he looked, more knowledgeable about his flowers and everything to do with these, so even in their sponges, she felt, older women were more expert, they showed a greater choice.

She laughed. They had more need of them than me, she said of older people and their dresses, but then they have no real need for better sponges. And then she saw everyone in the world, as the years went round and they grew older, becoming more and more careful in their choice, always refining, that is the nice ones.

There was mother for instance. Being an only child she'd been the chief person mother had lavished on. And as she walked down Oxford Street and saw all these provincial women in their mauves and browns she felt in a blaze her own position, where she was.

She sees where she is.

For the way she had been brought up was quiet, quiet. Where they lived in Kent no noise came to them but it was softened by distances and by the trees and the wind: when any noise came in by their tall windows it no more than murmured round her room. Where their house was in London a drumming noise was all they faintly heard: in Oxford Street the traffic clamored but where they lived not far away nothing was left of it, only a buzz of what went on there.

In Kent their house was Queen Anne, in London Adam. Her mother came up to London in February and left it in July to go down to Kent again. Weekdays her father was a city man, weekends a squire. All through the year he stayed Monday to Friday in his Adam house, Friday to Monday in his Queen Anne.

In the gardens at their house in Kent were hothouses, and, when her mother brought her up in February, flowers were sent to London for them. It was only when her mother was in town that Mr. Igtham had one vase of flowers in his room. Their name was Igtham. But Mrs. Igtham was most fond of flowers and her room was crammed with them, in banks up against the green-blue walls. Constance, her name is Constance, did not have so many. In her room they were put in old-fashioned silver vases, and they were put separately about, there were no great masses of them.

Always, wherever she went, Mrs. Igtham had blocks of flowers tightly packed against the walls, she was devoted to them. All round the year, whether she was in Kent or in London, her room was full of flowers so when you came in you were in a smother of them. She would be sitting plumb in the middle, not quite unlike a beetle. But Constance was not like that. If Mrs. Igtham, with all her rings and jewels—not that she ever looked to have too many—if Mrs. Igtham made you think she might have been a beetle, all sparkle in Garden of Eden, then Constance, to see her in her own room, looked really a silver lance sunk in the blue sea, in her blue-colored room.

Mrs. Igtham was a small dark blackish woman. She wore as jewelry mostly red stones and put more jewels about her than is usually done now, but, in her case, without its ever seeming odd. Having such a deal of stones glittering suddenly about her here and there, and being so dark, so with her it was like that glittering armored sheath above a beetle's wings: she might, when you saw her in the middle of her flowers, suddenly burst out flying, that sheath might suddenly burst open on her sharp and iridescent skin—she constantly wore black, she might at moments ride a broomstick.

Not so Mr. Igtham. Their name was correctly pronounced only by those who said Eyetam, not Iggetam or Iththam. He was fat and cared very much for shooting. Also he was a good businessman and served on boards of many companies. Everyone knew him and his wife, and these two did not go out of their way to know anyone. Constance was most of their link with other people, she went everywhere and was everyone's bridesmaid. Constance was utterly charming. This book is about Constance. When you have read it you too will say how charming Constance is.

As it was like saying Bellevoir or Burkeley to lisp Iththam, so you will appreciate that for centuries Igthams had lived in a delightful ease. In the eighteenth century they had been a great family of the church, three of them had been bishops at that time. Before then England, in the larger histories, in a historian's deep research, had cause to thank the Igthams. They had been a great landed family. Nor were they in that position now when a man might point at someone in the public baths and say: that

boy's family once ruled this island when England was most prosperous of all, five hundred years ago. For the Igthams had stayed
prosperous. They had gone into commerce. They were now rich,
but not too rich. They had a butler and a footman, a good cook—
yet she was not too good a cook—and these two lovely houses.

Her father's room looked to be what he was, comfortable and
prosperous, also a country gentleman. The walls were done in a
brown paper and on them hung pictures of horses which might be
by Alken or Sartorius. There was a big desk on which were many
papers and that one yellow china vase of flowers. It had flowers
in it only when Mrs. Igtham was in London. That vase was very
ugly and faded, chipped and old, but he held it in a great affection
because he could remember where it stood when he was small and
his nurse was washing him and tickling him. Was no telephone in
the room, that was outside, in a room of its own. These two things
were Mr. Igtham. His work he kept so to speak at an arm's length
away from him and he worshiped his childhood and his parents
in that vase. If a maid, in dusting, knocked it down and chipped
another fragment off it, then he was always very angry. His wife
used to say that she had never arrived at making him throw the
thing away, and she used to threaten him she would break the
horror, but as things were she was proud of him that he still kept
it. If now, this moment, he had thrown that vase down on purpose
and smashed it then she would have felt that he was not much
longer for this world. She would have had to eat all her flowers
then to keep a balance in the home.

When you came in by the front door, there, in the hall, were
flowers, only from February to July of course, vast bowl of them on
the hall table where lay two or three bowler hats of Mr. Igtham's.
Was a glass tray also, in which were cards. Then, quite often, under
the staircase on a huge table, were large cardboard boxes. From
these a sweet sticky smell came. They were boxes of flowers sent
up from Kent and waiting there for Mrs. Igtham to unpack them.
She would unpack them, marshal and mass them, make them
form fours, execute a great flanking movement round the corner
of her room with them, and here they would be, freshly cut, ready
for her lily hand. When she had done she would find Constance
and give her what was left over and tell her to arrange them for
her own rooms.

Constance had had no education in needlework or looking after babies or counting. She could talk French well. But she had never been to cooking classes or young conservative unions, Mrs. Igtham had never sent her and said go there and learn. And Constance would never have gone on her own. She chose her own dresses and arranged her own flowers, but she did not choose the decoration of her room. She had never ordered dinner. Mrs. Igtham thought, and who'll say she was wrong? thought that girls wanted no more than that, that need be all their accomplishment. Constance could read any book she liked and there you were, cultured, arranging her own flowers and dressing herself, why more? said Mrs. Igtham.

Her sitting room, then, was Mrs. Igtham's doing. Constance had no hand in it. In this room were four plain white pillars which went from floor to ceiling. On the blue walls were a number of old paintings, not good, not bad. Was a lot of yellow furniture about. On one side two long great windows lit this glittering room and by one of these, the nearest to the fire, was her writing table. The fireplace was Adam with two fluted marble pedestals. In front of this was a deep bearskin rug, the head left on. Mouth open it had a dry, red ink-colored tongue and gums and dull blue eyes but huge fangs, gloriously white and it was a polar bear. On the fireplace a great many invitation cards were propped up against the back and some letters, was a shining brass clock, old and Dutch, two Delft candlesticks and, on the right-hand edge of it what was really Constance, two small light painted aeroplanes in wood.

Lord when you came into that room and looked round and cried out, as you couldn't help doing, Lord what a fine room, then, when you saw those aeroplanes you might sing those are her pets, that's what is most hers in here. When you came in and saw them it might be like you came into a King's rooms and saw a local paper there. Or, more like, the other way about. You came into a common sort of room and then you saw two Kings seated by the fire.

These aeroplanes were old now, they were stained, and they'd never been any better than a child's toys. But Constance had bought them when she was no longer tiny, she'd bought them when she was nineteen. She had never played with them but she had put them there, she would have no one move them. And as she walked in Oxford Street, while her fancy walked like a blue cat about her room, the bright shining silver vases, her Dutch painted yellow chairs with flowers painted on them, the Dutch candlesticks, blue, such a lovely blue, then, standing on the polar bear, then again she met her aeroplanes and it was like where every year she'd gone since she was nineteen, the Mediterranean sea.

As you came down the beach so when you got into the sea it was like you had a halo round you, where the sun had been and now the warm sea lapped you, you felt you could roll like dolphins for that round fat feeling. Oh she had gone plunging out, her wet rubber cap had shone like any god, there were no waves, nothing but this blue sea, she rolled on it, the sun played like cymbals on her flanks and on one breast and then from a surfeit of all this she'd lain on her back and floated. She'd closed her eyes. But then was a hum like thousands cheering miles away and she looked and up above in that tremendous blue there was an aeroplane, aluminum-painted, all along its wings winking blinding light, high, high above, ever so slowly moving quite straight, like a Queen.

So when she came back to England she'd bought the model aeroplanes, aluminum-painted, because she'd been alone the time she saw that one from the sea, and because each time she was alone that was how she wanted it, how she'd always like to be.

She walks in Oxford Street.

Nobody would ever know, she sang as she looked about her in Oxford Street, no one, not one of these, not even mother, nobody would know about those aeroplanes. And when mother had had the walls done that gorgeous blue then suddenly she'd seen she could bring her Queens down from where she'd put them, in a drawer in her bedroom. But when she'd brought them down and put them on the mantelpiece (she'd put them on the same side one with the other because they looked nicer like that—one just poking in front of the other), when she'd stepped back to look, then she saw they weren't Queens anymore, but where they were now they were Kings.

Oxford Street blazed with the sun. There had been long
drought and grass in the Park was khaki-colored, which made
leaves on the plane trees look blue. The Marble Arch was white,
white. From wooden blocks which paved the roadway oozed tar in
which these blocks had been steeped, so, as a drunkard breathes
out the smell of what he has been drinking, so the smell of creosote
lay over where she walked. But as a drunkard, when he walks
about, may be withdrawn into himself, so she, filled with the heady
wine of Kings, stepped as though she had divinity about her, as
though heat, tar, and the crowds were nowhere near her, in her
companionship with mighty things.

As she slowly walked the people divided. Everyone made way
for Miss Igtham. She went between mothers and their children,
between sisters, between friends. Any men there were about took a
look at her because she was beautiful, particularly now. She wasn't
very tall but she had a most lovely body. She walked exactly like
herons fly. She was lightly dressed and as she walked it was the
balance, the assurance of movements which made you watch her.
For was nothing much about her face, and she was far lighter col-
ored than her mother. Her skin was creamier, it was a good face
to draw being fat and round but was nothing remarkable about
it except her eyelids were turned up at the outside corners. So
all the people were not merely looking at her features, it was the
majesty she had just assumed whilst walking, it was her tread, her
magnificence which marked her.

She walked absorbed. And if you had passed your hand over
her skin it would have dragged at your fingers. The sun, in crashing
down, had opened her pores, each one had opened like it might
be flowers in the sun. So for a time she walked, as when in the
warm sea the water is exactly at that heat where you forget you
have a body. Also she had these dreams I have described.

But she came back. The sun became too hot for her before
she had gone far, and as a good diver will dive into the flat sea
to come up again and break the surface with less than one quiver
over the water, so she returned. Immediately she thought about
her dress. And at once she turned back, immediately thinking she
must go to the Park and sit there, under a plane tree.

This morning she had no ploy, no shopping, nothing to pass
the time. Suddenly she was depressed. She crossed over to other

side of the street, into the shade, and begged that her shoes might not be ruined by the tar.

Everyone she passed she hated now, and she felt her dress was not sitting right. She longed for nothing more than to get quickly to the Park, she'd have given anything for someone to offer a lift. It was not far enough for a penny bus ride, it wouldn't take a minute to walk, but still why couldn't that idiot Eddy be close by with his Lea Francis. Oh, she cried out to herself, it made you frantic, this useless walking.

II

She sees what she used to be.

When she sat down not far from the Marble Arch, under a plane tree she arranged her dress. She pulled at it at her hip and spread it out to her knees, then at last she felt comfortable again. The damp heat of the day grew over her and then once more she was dreaming. And as in the warm sea the water is sometimes exactly at that heat where you forget you have a body so she might have been floating in the Mediterranean sea, lain on her back.

She swooned. People were riding about on those pneumatic horses made of rubber, the pink rubber whales, and unicorns, on the water. Their cries as they played had faintly reached her, all softened by the expanse. And she thought of when she was small, when as children they had been playing in the hay meadows.

In those days, when she was nine years old, another girl of her age, called Celia, was educated with Miss Igtham. This girl lived with them in Kent, her parents were in India, and shared the French governess hired for Constance.

In those days, every afternoon at three, they had gone out walking. This day their governess took them down to the hay meadows.

Mademoiselle wore white stockings and white kid shoes with high, high heels. On top she had a vast straw hat. She held a big black bag close to her. Except for these she was very small, not so very much taller than they, and she walked in tiny steps. One on each side of her, each of them holding one of her arms in their two hands—she had white cotton gloves to her elbows, they shouted across her to each other, never in French always in English, and she was always away in her thoughts. She did not hear what they said because she would fix all her attention onto keeping clean her shoes, and on her balance, which was precarious on those heels like stilts.

When they left the road it was harder than ever for her to get along. The children would hop and skip while they held on to her arms and she felt the grass was crawling with what she loathed more than any living thing, ants. But they had persuaded her to let them watch the hay being made because she had seen an opportunity in it to sit under a hedge at her ease. Even sitting on an ant-heap was better than the walk along these enervating roads which went meandering like streams, monuments to waste. And while she sat they could play and as they ran while they played so they would get so much the more exercise than if she had walked with them. And then again her heart at that time was heavy for Dreyfus. She longed to be back in France while this case was going on, to be at the center of things.

When they realized the meadow men there were carting the hay, sun was so fierce that there was a danger the hay would be burnt. The children were sad that they were taking it away so soon. But they planned a game where it still lay as it had been cut and afterwards turned, in great concentric rings, in golden dykes with the blue grass like flowing in between.

Mademoiselle went to the near corner of this meadow into the shade of an ash tree. Graciously this tree reached out olive-blue branches and poured shade on the ground. Here were two horses harnessed to an empty farm wagon. The sun, striking down between the leaves in tubes, hit their coats in little egg-shaped patches. Flies bothered them. Every now and again one or the other would half kick out and so rattle the chains, and they kept sawing their heads and so jingled the harness.

Mademoiselle took from her bag a copy of *The Times* and opening this out she sat down on it as far as she might away from the horses without leaving the shade. She did not rest her back but sat erect, hands folded on her lap, and then, once she was settled, she disappeared completely. For the horses had deep-colored coats which bayed like tigers from the deep shade out at the sunlight, and she was nothing beside the heavy wagon painted a low, crude blue.

Constance and Celia went to where the men were working in a knot about the other wagon, loading it. Two men stood on the hay in the wagon while the others pushed hay along with their forks till they had a sufficiency before them. Then they dug the forks in and with the one movement they heaved their forkload to the two who waited to receive it on the wagon, and these packed that hay in. As the wagon was filled and became stacked up with hay so these two rose higher and higher on it: Constance and Celia watched their red faces and red arms, and listened, as one of them was singing. But they soon wandered off, tired of watching.

Mademoiselle was nodding and was soon quite lost in a doze.

The children couldn't decide at first what they would play. So they sat down and plaited hay into pigtails till they should think of something. They laughed and giggled. And meanwhile the wagon had been filled and stacked, and those two men on top had roped it. Each taking hold on one of these ropes, they had slid down, and now all the men went to shade of that ash tree where the governess was and that other wagon. The noise of their coming woke her and while one of them was finding the cider she passed the time of day with them. Then they offered her a hornful of cider and she drank the clear yellow, thinking of their farm at home. It was bitter to her taste. It made the back of her neck burn, and she laughed and thanked them. She forgot ants. She lay back even and propped her chin on her arm. The heavy sweet scent of the hay came like honey to her and the smell of these men's bodies made her homesick. The horses were strong too, the whole summer's day was reeking and she was most deliciously overcome, clinging to consciousness as to the last firm thing on earth. The men sat nearby and one was so amused he lay shaking on his back, hands pressed to his belly, while another wanted to give the children cider, but the rest would not let him.

Constance next found a short stick among the hay and began playing with it, first putting it about her body. At last she suddenly put that stick to her head. She put it flat with her forehead, so it stuck up above her hair like a horn. And at once she thought of unicorns. In lessons they had come upon them, on the pages of their book, pacing along a ride trampling the flowers. Celia remembered. And so they played at being unicorns.

Celia found a stick and first they walked on the new grass between the golden dykes of hay and then they ran along these long concentric rings. Each round they made, one following the other, brought them nearer to the middle of this piece which had been mowed in a round.

The horses harnessed to the full wagon followed them with their wide eyes from where they had been left not far away. The children ran shrieking round and then, as they neared the center, they grew more quiet. The horses shifted, they would turn their heads away and yet always come back to the children. The men, sitting low in shade, lazily watched them, only the governess paid no attention. And as they came nearer and nearer in to the center, in ever-shortening circles, those two horses, hidden from the men by their wagon, grew more uneasy. They snorted through their wide nostrils, distended and red. The children came nearer and nearer in: each horse struck at the ground, their quarters trembled, they were thrown into a sweat. And when at last the center was reached and the children fell down there both of them with what came to the men as a faint cry then those two horses, with a scream, bolted. They careered away, the wagon pitching, crashing behind them.

Then the men surged out of the deep shade and ran after them in a fumbling group, running and shouting. Mademoiselle also came out, she wavered out towards the children. They, for their part, sat terrified and Constance could remember now how she had thought that they were blameless, she could remember reminding herself then that Mademoiselle had only told them to be sage, or wise.

Sitting near the Marble Arch she opened her eyes. The world struck white at her, for two moments she was so dazzled that everything appeared like wraiths, or as an image of what was real. People shimmered by, walking on the path she was close to. But when at last everyone took on their true shape and all the rumble of the traffic reoccupied her ears—before it had been the surf on her seashore—then she fell to watching.

Listless, she watched them pass, young and old, old and young, children, soldiers, beggars, dogs, a monkey, nurses with prams.

Young couples went by, today was a holiday, and only these had that glaring look of Kings in all their gentleness.

And then she thought of couples—why in a moment, she cried in her heart, they might break out and play, any second now for their own amusement they may take on the parts of unicorns or Kings. And perhaps that was why so many people kept dogs, who can never have enough of your love if they are yours, who will always play with you, for food or love you are Queens to them, Kings.

A woman will take a walk with her dog and it will keep her pleasantly distracted. As they walk their two perceptions will be allied, when she stops to turn something over with her stick he will come back from where he has run out in front to examine it with her, when he turns to the long grass and brambles she will cheer him on and watch after his efforts.

So two people who love each other can go out and as they walk there is no need for them to put anything into words, having expressed everything long ago. As they walk, and the countryside meanders by, they need not be looking at the same things, one may be looking to her right the other to her left, but still their thoughts are most curiously joined and what they both see says but the one same thing to them.

When Constance and Celia had walked on either side of Mademoiselle they had said always what first came into their heads. They had no withdrawals one from the other, any whim, any little thing, anything whatever they immediately told. Then when they had grown up there were a very few they hadn't told each other, each had just one or two reservations, but they had already said so much that when they went out walking it was in a great lassitude of silence, a delicious boredom. Constance laughed. For now Celia was married Constance had lost her, when they were together now they avoided silence and said easy things rather quickly to each other.

Your dog dies and after a little you buy another, your friend goes and if you are lucky you find a new friend. And all the time you are learning to walk alone. When Celia married she had gone the way of all other friends. When you have been two you can't be three and now Constance was alone. Celia had married Eddy two years ago and now Constance had no one so to speak to play with.

Everyone ought to play she thought. She looked at the beggars, the soldiers, the young and old, and there was a woman with that same high voice. If she played ever she would cry from nerves. And yet she would put her legs over a rubber unicorn, better than no unicorn at all only it was a kind of sacrilege, and go bobbing out on the sea. But Constance had no call to use rubber unicorns. And that woman would not go far out, she would be yelling and shrieking like any housemaid, and she would soon be back under that vast umbrella she had pitched for her. She thought, and drew comfort from it, how that woman's life was too full, how she would never be able to walk down Oxford Street her fingers about his horn, her unicorn, arm along his neck, for she would never in her thoughts be alone enough for him.

And Celia also had lost all semblance of what she had been. Constance laughed and thought if they were to go back together now to the Mediterranean again as they had done before Celia married, Constance thought how different it would be. Although she had been alone when that aeroplane came overhead yet she had bought two aeroplanes, one loneliness for each of them. She had not told Celia about it. They had often swum out together, she had been glad to draw Celia away from the beach, they had lain side by side dazed by the sun and delight out on the sea. So Constance had bought one for herself and one for Celia as a celebration in honor of those occasions. And Constance, who had looked on the aeroplanes as one and the same and had held neither in preference one to the other, had chosen one of the two for her very own when Celia married, a secret one.

She was now in the position of someone whose friend has gone and who goes walking alone, gleefully swiping down grass at her side with her stick. And now that reserve which had, in one or two things, been between them, now that also was gone since Celia was no longer with her. Now she was completely alone there was no restraint at her heart and she could walk proudly.

For sitting in the heavy night in the gardens of their hotel, over the sea, every foot of ground quivering with the shrill cicadas, the heavy night where every tree breathed on her and drooped down from where it had reached up back down to earth and the low noise of the sea, from the cackle of lights she saw through the leaves, she heard Celia laughing.

Once Constance had walked across the School Yard at Eton, and it was deserted, when she had heard such another laugh and had turned round in joy, singing, isn't that gorgeous in a place built in fear like this. So when she heard Celia laugh she remembered.

And she had felt oh how can she laugh like that, why should she bring the playing fields here, and she had hidden her eyes in her warm fingers.

She had stayed on that seat it seemed like hours, not daring to move in case she came across them. And why, she thought with even now a small pang, why should things one has enjoyed come flying back like a bent withy and strike one and hurt, why should things turn inside out.

She had heard Celia laugh again then, and for a moment she had thought they were coming straight down on her and then she'd heard her laugh again, this time halfway down the rocks and to the sea. She had cried, nothing had ever been so bitter, cried and cried till she lost all count, while the earth shrilled and the trees moaned with the weight of thick leaves on them.

That had been the last time they had been together to the Mediterranean for Celia had married that man. And now Constance could laugh at all that, only the way she laughed it made hardly any sound at all, being like a soft neigh at the back of her throat.

For before that last year they had gone out under the moon, under the trees, the palm trees with thousands of birds sleeping above in them so it seemed because they were never altogether still, in the beating night with the earth crying out in the cicadas, where the trees heaved down in the night air which was like bed, they had sat there in a trance when they were younger than they were now, three years ago.

They had gone to the outmost edge of the garden and lights over that porch which led to the hotel were caught in a tiny reflection in their glasses on the marble table which gleamed like skin in the dark. They sat on a bench which had been made to encircle a tree, when they leaned back the bark, which was not hot or cold, pressed into their backs in long furry tongues. The marble table kept a hoard of coolness and their glasses of the dark wine looked like huge soft eyes, the pair of them, marvelously soft.

In those nights, hand in hand, they had gone silently sailing and voices from the veranda way away and the low noise of the sea had come faintly like a small wind to take them further out on dreams. They had gone slipping out and once Constance had stumbled on Celia's pulse and had gone beating out on that into a smother of dreams, a glorious obscurity.

Or again they had climbed from the beach up in the evening by the path which was cut out of the cliff, it went in large flat spirals, and while they were always chattering when they began to climb it by the time they were halfway up they had never any breath left for talk. Constance had come in the daytime, so she remembered, to hope that this bliss they had then would be renewed each night. For when darkness first showed in the sky after the sun was gone it was then every evening they began their climb.

When they had to stop they flung their arms about each other and would turn out over the Mediterranean to see that shadow coming in over the water like a sleep. Constance laughed as she remembered. She held Celia tight and in her she embraced that enchantment, all the colors marching night made on the sea and what it is to stand on a cliff and watch. But at the first chill that reached them of that shadow they turned again and slowly climbed up till by the time they had set foot on the lowest terrace of the gardens night was rushing by above them, flying with the speed of the world and with the speed of the sun.

At that moment a girl laughed as she went along on the path in front of Constance. No one could laugh, in the mood Constance was now, without her looking up, for as she was now laughter ran like blue threads in her blue tapestry, the fabric of her dreams. But this girl sounded like she must be tired and Constance marveled again at how little the English love heat, for all they talk about it, and decided that they preferred sharp, frosty weather. Certainly this ticket collector did, she said to herself, and followed him with her eyes as he came towards her. He came slowly along, walking splayfooted, dragging his heels, and he had his uniform cap pushed onto back of his head, and the curve of his forehead showed many bumps in it. He was fifty, his eyes were gray, and he was a very small man. Constance thought he did look so ill.

This man longed for the night. Then, when the shadows came flowing out of trees again all over the ground, and the grass opened its eyes, when the lamps were lit he would soon be able to make his way home then. It was the uniforms that did it and he spent much of his time in hoping that the man who designed his uniform and the tailor who made it might one day have to wear the lousy thing that was more meant for a fireman than a man that had to keep moving. It would be all right for one whose job let him stand on a ladder with the flames licking round him and play a hose onto it and when he got down everyone saying hero, hero, but was none of that talk about when he got home, with his feet feeling like he had been walking on embers all the long day. Not much. Yes and you felt dizzy too with it, nor you didn't dare have a sit, they were down on you so sharp, or an old man wrote to the papers. And why should people pay for sitting, wasn't it mean of them that charged it, for the Parks did ought to be free, or they should put more free seats about. Yes, he said, it made you kind of miserable to be always doing a thing which went against your nature but then why there was some you didn't mind dunning, there was that piece over there, she was so rich she ought to pay. You didn't mind taking her pence, nor nobody wouldn't as you could see from here she filled the eyes: and he slowly bore down on Constance.

Constance opened her bag to look for her purse. In the end she had to take out her handkerchief and pay more attention to what she was doing. Standing above her he held the ticket in his fingers and Lord love us he thought if women don't put a lot in there. But he found his eyes followed the line of her left hand which held the bag while she fumbled in it with her right, and if, automatically almost, he kept exclaiming within him at the magnificence of that blue cigarette case and God help us look at that holder, yet the major part of him yearned to an exquisite transparency, like a seashell in the sea, where her thumb branched off from the palm of her hand. Save us, he cried out in his heart, if I couldn't bury my nose in there, such fine hands, never a day's work in their lives, and the nails, like a quartz.

Can't you find it miss he said hopefully and she said oh dear and took out that cigarette case out of the way. Let me hold it miss and she said yes do, giving it to him without looking up. He held it and now he was lost, for he began to wonder what it was like inside as he held that case all of a glisten in his hand. His eyes turned from her and he put his two hands to the case so that it lay on his two palms. And so closely did he watch it that when at last she held out his pennies to him she had to say I'm so sorry before he knew she was ready, so that he all but dropped the thing from embarrassment as he gave it back to her. So stupid of me, she said, I'm so sorry, she apologized again, but he had nothing he could find to say. What a pair of eyes, he was laughing inside him, what a grand pair of blue eyes for a man to see he laughed.

He had looked into her eyes. She had looked into his. She had seen a light of mockery there. As she had seen that monkey go careering down along the path in front of her, so Constance, being like she was this day, had invested that collector with another life, a new agility. Being so lovely she had brought him out of himself like the night would do which he longed for so: that light in his eye was almost as she had been with Celia on their rocks on the Mediterranean sea. But he was a man. She felt he had been half mocking at her for being a woman. She had a small creepy feeling at that, like her senses were coiled up inside.

These things coming to her about him made her petulant with the collector who, so it seemed, had mocked at her King. Spitefully she watched him move away. What was so shocking in monkeys was that they were nearly human, what was dreadful in men was their similarity to apes. He had been very insolent, she thought now, and would have liked to wake him: if he had tried one thing too much, if he had exceeded in any way at all, then she would have dropped on him. Instead she had apologized. She laughed. It was too squalid, she kept thinking, squalid saying I'm sorry to him when it was so really lucky for that man to see me and so to refresh his eyes.

For when he had come up to her she had shared her glory with him. Part of the time his attention had been taken up with the things she had about her, that was true, but it was no less true that when their eyes met his eyes received that glare of Kings. Even though he'd had to stand away and mock he'd had it. But it was as though you took up that flat spiraled path and you turned him to face out over the sea, and then he cared for nothing but eating. Looking out over the Mediterranean he would see no food, but feeling you beside him and that you cared for what you saw there, then a mocking light came out in his eye because of you. And this collector, when he had seen her happy, had thought if he'd been luckier he might have had a bit then—that was her opinion of his look now she thought of it.

People are most of all indulgent when they are happy and she had shared her glory with him when she had caught his eye. When he'd seen it he must have thought why shouldn't I come in under the wing of that, damn him. He had felt she was so occupied with Kingship that anyone who put himself forward just then she would mistake for Kings, that the majesty she had on her was so great she could see nothing small or mean, that a mercy had made her infinitely indulgent since she had climbed so high and was so majestically detached.

She watched a couple pass before her. They had on them a mood so gentle that everything was brother, sister to them. They had that in the way Kings could be proudly apart and yet near to the people. But it was the loneliness in high places which was the great memory you could have, those secret walks with pets where there were no men to ape cheeky monkeys, that was what counted.

Oh being a King was really for when you were alone, for that was the only kind that lasted. You could promise, you could swear, but friends nearly always changed as the years went round. They married, or one might go to Africa to shoot big game and then stay there drinking, or another was sent to Mexico, and there were convents. Everywhere you looked were graves for friendship, love, and tombstones on everyone's tongue.

Of everyone you met was only you you would be with always, and she thought that's how it is, don't let's have any monkey business with other people, the issue ultimately is with ourselves. As my two eyes are coordinated so let me have myself as my friend, may I have that glory where I draw on no one, lean on nobody. May I learn to be alone.

Olein

Maud worshiped Vincent. Vincent teased Maud. In the '20s, the conversation in grand English country houses was always about apples, and in this excerpt, recorded by their eighteen-year-old son, Henry, neither he nor their guest Olein, an unknown visiting foreign cousin, can get a word in edgeways.

—Sebastian Yorke

Coming in to dinner

VINCENT YORKE

The first apples!

MAUD YORKE

Oh Lord. Olein don't eat one or you'll be made to go miles up to the farm to look at apple trees.

VINCENT

My dear I only try to please. No Olein do eat one, you'll find them better than any of these things they import from abroad. Try one now, it doesn't matter about the soup.

MAUD

No really Vincent do let us live like civilized beings. Of course Olein can't eat an apple before her soup.

VINCENT

Well my dear as we all know, you never take any and I thought Olein wouldn't mind. You don't mind do you Olein. I'm going to take one even if no one else does.

MAUD

Oh no Vincent I can't allow this. It is like savages and their pig tub. If only Norbury would give me the horse and cart, instead of bringing apples down here I could get some coke in. The peaches will all die, there is no heat in the greenhouses.

[*By this time they are all drinking soup except* MAUD]

VINCENT

I hate your indoor peaches. Besides my dear surely you have lived long enough in the country to know this is haymaking time.

MAUD

Haymaking, fiddlesticks. Well eat up your soup quick then. I am hungry. Eaton bring the fish in please.

VINCENT

Oh and now it will be cold. My dear do have some regard for others. It isn't fair, is it Olein, and our little man won't like his dinner. But then I'm afraid he never does.

MAUD

Henry has got a great flair for food. When we were in France together he always ordered the best dishes.

VINCENT

Everything he does is right. Olein I hope you don't spoil your nephews and nieces in the way that my wife spoils her sons.

MAUD

Anyway she doesn't insist on them eating apples with the soup.

VINCENT

How do you know dear, you have never stayed in the wild part of the world she lives in. They shoot you there if you go out.

MAUD

My dear Vincent that joke is quite played out. Olein I wanted to ask you, how does your mother get the coke for her gardens?

VINCENT

Maud dear, don't ask these questions. From the coal merchant of course.

MAUD

Don't interrupt me. It wasn't only that I wanted to know. I asked what the lawyers call a leading question.

VINCENT

Then I don't think it's polite. Anyway leading questions aren't allowed in the law. A leading question as we all know is to prompt unfairly. I don't know what they taught you when you were young. Olein we are treating you very badly. By Jove these *petits pois* are wonderful. What food you do get in the country.

MAUD

Wodehouse don't be so greedy, there won't be none left for us. As for leading questions damn the law courts.

VINCENT

My dear don't use such language, it pains me.

MAUD

Oh Billy look you have let the *petits pois* slip right down your shirtfront. Sit still while I wipe it off for you. I am afraid the shirt's ruined.

VINCENT

Oh my dear don't be so gloomy. Can't I afford a new one?

MAUD

Well that is the first time since we married that I've heard you talk about getting a new shirt.

VINCENT

Olein is that fair, I ask you, when she spends £500 a year on her clothes?

MAUD

Oh humph.

VINCENT

Yes it's all very well, my dear, you make noises at me, but I'm economical, I don't spend money like water as you do.

MAUD

Wodehouse don't try and get a rise out of me. I am tired tonight.

VINCENT

Shall we have some champagne in honor of Olein's visit?

MAUD

Oh Billy that would be nice, it would do me worlds of good.

Biographical Note

Sixty years ago, a well-born Englishman named Henry Yorke could usually be found at lunchtime in the London office of his family's engineering firm, writing. After Eton and Oxford, he had joined the business on the shop floor and had risen to become managing director. In conventional terms, he was leading a successful enough life, and he and his wife were an attractive, amusing couple, popular in London society. Their circle was large and glamorous, the Bright Young Things and the Oxford Wits of the 1920s and '30s: Aly Khan, the Guinnesses, Lady Ottoline Morrell, the Mitford and Lygon sisters, writers like Anthony Powell and Evelyn Waugh, fashionable dons such as Maurice Bowra, and, later, the painter Matthew Smith.

But the managing director of H. Pontifex & Sons in some ways stood outside this world: partly because he was a businessman, but also because of the unusual character of what he was writing at his desk in the middle of the day. The books Henry Yorke worked on at the office were among the most distinctive novels of his time. He thought that to be known as a novelist might harm him in business, so he published them under a pseudonym: Henry Green.

Green wrote nine novels: *Blindness, Living, Party Going, Caught, Loving, Back, Concluding, Nothing,* and *Doting.* In their teasing, wry comprehensiveness, the titles do not mislead. Each book is different from the others, but they all have an instantly recognizable signature of tone. They draw on apparently irreconcilable contemporary styles: the experimental modernism of James Joyce, Virginia Woolf, and Wyndham Lewis; the social realism of James Hanley and Edward Upward; the high-society comedy of Evelyn Waugh and Anthony Powell. If the blend had been less individual, it might have been repudiated by all these camps. But since his early twenties, Green had been recognized as a distinctive and bold artist in his own right. He could lay on words as Van Gogh could paint (the sunburnt hay in "Mood," spread out "in great concentric rings, in golden dykes with the blue grass like flowing in between"). Yet his human attentiveness was as self-effacing as Chekhov's.

This attentiveness is partly a matter of his acute and impartial ear. But he heard people's dreams, as well as their words. Eudora Welty wrote that he turned what people say "into the fantasy of what they are telling each other, at the same time calling up out of their own mouths their vital spirit." This sounds, and can be, romantically intense. But Green is also a very funny writer. His books are classics of modern comedy, and they might find more readers if this were more often said.

His sympathy and his hilarity are both found in the fragments published here. The combination made the man as strange as his writing. At his memorial service in 1973, V. S. Pritchett spoke of his "spirit of poetry, fantasy and often wild laughter"—*spirit*, again, as if Green (throughout the long last years of his fictional silence a difficult, moody figure, a heavy drinker, and a recluse) had seemed to his friends an Ariel, bringing transformation out of the offices of Pontifex & Sons, a short walk from where Constance dreams her life in "Mood."

His working there was in part an act of piety to his entrepreneurial father, Vincent Yorke. Fortunately, he didn't follow him in everything. When Henry began writing at school, Vincent showed his stuff to the adventure-novelist John Buchan, on whose advice he recommended that his son give it up. It's clear from "Olein" how keenly Henry could listen to his parents, without heeding them. But his father's disapproval of the novels and of their lack of commercial success galled him: he would have liked his books to sell.

In 1959 Green was to describe "Mood" as a second novel that he had been unable to complete. His early mentor, the Oxford literary critic Nevill Coghill, wrote to him, "Your new book *Meretricity* [the original title for "Mood"] is very ambitious, and if you succeed in it, as you have in *Blindness* and *Living*, it will have been worth all your depression about it." This is its first appearance in the United States. "Olein" is the shortest of several dramatic pieces and has never been printed before. Both are among a trove of scarcely examined manuscripts and letters on which I have been working in the hope of writing the author's biography. They now belong to Henry Green's son, Sebastian Yorke, by whose permission they appear.

—Jeremy Treglown

FRIEDERIKE MAYRÖCKER

Heiligenanstalt

1

"so strongly pulled down by the neck" (Clara to Brahms) "the love-
liest wires and butterfly chest (letter slope) short-lived from room
wire to room wire"
(whereupon Brahms cabled) "precisely" (and) "the wires, Clara:
an autopsy would reveal sublime psychodramas, navels with billboards and smokestacks. But you are secretly a *child of nature.*
Whereas I have an irrepressible urge to make my body carry to
painful term all that goes against my psyche."
"Your static intelligence, or penchant for idylls. Do tell me."
whereas a bit of Eichendorff.

2

"there is a reason, dear Clara, for what may seem an arbitrary
preference for following your example, as it were, in alternating
forms of address: it's because you seem at the same time close and
distant" (Brahms to Clara).
(Clara in any case not) fitted waist.
"and thus" (Clara to Brahms) "invoking some dark temptation we
kept fretting for what seemed forever."
"Robert, however, resolutely progresses in his illness."
"as if taking leave."
"when Robert, still at the gate, waved the bunch of flowers I had
brought."
"then we gave up, *and so disappeared* (as if going home)."

3

"insists on being left alone" (Clara to Brahms).
"then again claims he can only live holding my hand."
"in felt slippers, on tiptoe, over the shiny tiles, as if he didn't want
to make a sound."
"is no one! (torchbearer) Calif, and some flakes of snow."
"or such a paper May!"
"the terrible sounds he wheezes out—crackling fire."
when he came back, and her eyes dilated.

4

"take care" (Brahms to Clara) "that your phases of depression
don't follow too closely on one another."
"as if of oaks, his chest in the shadow of, his fissured hand" (Clara
to Brahms) "and how he, for the whole country, but in a vast quiet
field, assuaged by pain."
"precisely" (Brahms to Clara).
"can't you speak openly?" (Clara to Brahms) "do you have visitors?"

5

"as if a whole band of outsiders suddenly moved into your house
and held a 'surprise love-in, redeeming the next century'" (Clara
to Brahms).
"just imagine coming back and finding all those people gathered
in my house—a pandemonium."
"and to paint the rest of the guests the desired color" (Brahms to
Clara).
"one thing I must gripe about, I live in a veritable kitchen: sprout-
ing cabbage heads, tiny, with wrinkled skin, green veins, and the
bookshelves all raw."

"me the singing dilettante—spite-box piano."

"as if I hadn't ever composed a single note. As if I had stayed a mere dilettante."

6

"criteria of taste, however, I will not admit in this context" (Brahms to Clara).

"as the children come later" (Clara to Brahms), "darling morrow. Only hours between us."

"At times I'm tormented with self-reproach. But gravity makes me rush toward you, I cannot help it."

"room flooded with sun. We shouldn't confuse lies and truth" (Brahms to Clara).

"*well, you just let it happen!*" (Clara to Brahms).

7

(Clara in any case not) fitted waist.

"takes long trips on a map. And asks don't I see the contradiction of having fireworks by daylight" (Clara to Brahms).

"let's go down to the Rhine one last time" (Schumann to Clara).

"it will take me long to get used to the thought that I must take a different road now. Whose abyss, seclusion."

"our platonic household."

"*is he one of your little milk cows?*"

8

"the serene waters of resigned mourning" (Epistle to the Corinthians).

"it's one foot before the other, all in the dark" (Schumann to Clara).

"a fetus of a sound."
"trees falling heavy shadows."
"(Chivalry = seated on horses, same qualities. Falls. Epilepsy)."
"they *have* to close! on streets and bridges, including Lacy's grave."
"antler storm and 1 mystery."
"in French: thatched roof, roof skin (?)."
"sad that she has to disguise herself" (Schumann to Brahms).

9

in the park grounds, snow falling on his hair, his bare chest.
"the ash-gray pollen (octopus) in clouds over her face" (Schumann
to Brahms) "a veil."
"her bluish skin! so that I had trouble recognizing the familiar
features. But it was only the dark shadow of a tree where she
stopped for a moment before coming toward me."
"he was unsure in telling time" (Clara to Brahms).
"arms suddenly flailing, 40 days letter storm."
"later a board game in the garden."
"when we came out of the house, brief fright. Finger exercises,
substitute rain field."
when he came back, and her eyes dilated.

10

"gathered in you as focus!" (Clara to Brahms).
"but I shall have to flee you."
"no more emotional straining" (Brahms to Clara).
"a secret cannot be described; you never know if it is simple or
difficult" (Clara to Brahms).
"as soon as I am supposed to represent my experience, my life, all
incentive to go on composing is spoiled" (Brahms to Clara).

11

"a nearly frightening harmony" (Clara to Brahms), "as our associations run along the same lines at the same speed."
"Bull's-eye."
"it is as if the bombs had sought out the church" (Schumann to
Clara) "organ in flames."
"they *have* to close them! on streets and bridges, including the
northeast suburbs down the Rhine, touched-up sludge."
"compass needle, trembling in the half-light."

12

"the memory of this having-been-there-with-you" (Clara to Brahms),
"and how at the end you were up and gone in a second—while
I mechanically started home, not wanting to see what went on
around me, and at home wrote a few pages for you"—
"so much I wanted to tell you, say such nonsense."
"actually, not even 2 pianos are enough (Fauvistes)" (Brahms to Clara).
"The audience gape (scribble), *and how they all start clapping before
the cadenza is over!"*

13

DEW, mildewed Bastille.
"professional bent even without sons" (Brahms to Clara).
"bodily, wires" (Clara to Brahms).
(whereupon Brahms cabled) "read many books back then. Each
led to others with mysterious tips, leads, relations, which I was only
too glad to follow up."
"put all my money into books, from childhood on read as much
as I could and without guidance went all the way from the worst
to the best."

"can't get out of this spinning of fabulous fibrous fringe phantasies" (Clara to Brahms) "brooding for hours, *the whir of longing gaining speed.*"

14

"Things answer only when things want!" (Schumann to Clara) "the kitchen cabinet, drawer, sudden noise—(and don't know how to stop it)"
"until he discovers and drags them out into the light of day" (Clara to Brahms) "Echolalia: and hesitant, poison-wise."
"later pointed under the table, lifted the tablecloth. And said, faltering: here . . . and . . . over there . . . they're watching . . . all around us . . . behind . . . the curtains . . ."
"we took a long walk through the park. Flakes blown against his hair, his bare chest."
"he refused to put on a coat."

15

"the blackbird this morning" (Clara to Brahms) "at his window."
"ran mincingly back and forth, drumming on the sill with its beak."
"he wanted to copy it: knocked with both index fingers on the edge of the table, with violent syncopation: bad bird! bad bird!— growled in mock exaggeration: wanted to wake him! wanted to wake him! with mincing steps! wanted to wake him! no! no!—"
"what we've left is misshapen encounters" (Brahms to Clara).
"and where do you buy this beautiful staff paper?" (Schumann to Brahms).

16

"Sankt Gmunden—to get back up where I fell" (Brahms to Clara).
"bones filled with air" (Schumann to Clara) "my teeth huge erratic
boulders grinding away in my mouth."
"souls, or animals, bows and arrows from their bodies."
"3 wax tablets picturing the Paschal Lamb."
"dilettantism in any art is obvious to those who know: *where nothing*
is transformed, or too little" (Schumann to Brahms).

17

"sea mist, sharps and flats, a study in falling" (Clara to Brahms).
"around its funnel shape, the bend of the Rhine."
"I'm not sorry I didn't ask him."
"suddenly in the street" (Brahms to Clara) "I saw *your face, aged,* on
an old woman passing."
"it is like death, very close to the earth" (Clara to Brahms).
"Your shuddering, trembling—which are the transformations of
your love?"

18

"long days of gray sky, no stars and no sun" (Schumann to Clara).
"feel I write on the sky, fabricate lightning if the miracle meets
with disbelief, I dream of soil in spring, watch grave diggers, sweep
dust so senselessly."
"white sun in motion—your *flying finger-moons rising and setting in-*
side me."
"1 month ago in Africa and Johannesburg: astonishing cable!"
when he came back, and her eyes dilated.

19

"these sheets of music: my act of union with you" (Brahms to Clara).

"sat long in the North Star" (Schumann to Clara) "immovable feasts."

"*here they threw a sun over me,* lots of blossoms, I feel I'm flying."

"by settling all too close to the regions of phantasy" (Clara to Brahms) "we put forth make-believe blossoms, make-believe fruit." (whereupon Brahms cabled) "flowered fans streamlings, twice-baked!"

"something restless within the constant."

Translated by Rosmarie Waldrop

In the Land
of the Blind

At the time of the accident, the boy was about three years old. He was playing in the workshop of his father, a saddler in Coupvray, a French village on the Marne. He was alone, and no one knows exactly what happened. Playing with some tools, he poked himself with an awl or knife in the eye. The eyeball had been perforated and was irreparably damaged. In 1812, little medical assistance was available in cases of serious injury, especially in the country. Napoleon had set forth on his Russian campaign that summer, and hundreds of doctors were accompanying the army to Moscow. In the absence of any other treatment, people resorted to folk remedies, so the child's eye was dressed with medicinal plasters and herbs. A complication set in, causing blindness in the other eye as well; the infection may have spread from the injured eye, or the healthy eye may have been damaged by an unusual immunological response.

The child was plunged into permanent darkness. The parents did their best to raise the child, but they could see no future for him. The blind received no special assistance in those days, and if they had no family to take care of them, they had to earn their livelihood by begging or by being exhibited at fairs.

The boy was extremely intelligent and had a cheerful disposition. His saddler father, assisted by the family pastor, tried to teach him to read with letters made by hammering hobnails into pieces of wood. By touching these "alphabet blocks," the boy learned the letters and a few simple words. His father also taught him to write the letters on paper. But this did not help him with reading or writing at the village school, although he excelled in other subjects by virtue of his exceptional memory.

As a result of the Terror, much of France's limited experience in educating the blind had been lost. In 1771, a young official in Paris had given a few coins to a young, blind beggar outside a church. He noticed that the boy fingered the coins to assess their value. The official, Valentin Hauy, became a "Pygmalion" to the boy, whom he adopted, and devoted the rest of his life to the education of the blind. He began teaching the lad by using blocks of wood with letters carved on them in relief, but these were too crude and primitive to be useful for reading. Seeking a better solution, Hauy thought of raised print. If letters could be impressed on strong paper with enough force, they would appear in relief on the other side and fingers could feel them. Hauy immediately started soliciting funds and, in 1785, opened a small school in Paris for the blind, with his young pupil as the first teacher. The teaching materials consisted of a dozen books printed with the letters in relief. The Academy of Sciences took an interest, and the pupils demonstrated their finger-reading for Louis XVI and Marie Antoinette. The school was designated a royal institution, although that did not guarantee it any income. Then, during the Revolution, all vestiges of the ancien régime were swept away. The school ceased to exist, the blind children were scattered among workhouses and asylums, and Hauy fled France.

When the French monarchy was restored, the new king, especially concerned about the blind, sponsored the establishment of a Royal Institute for Blind Children, to which each region of France could send one child. The building made available to the institute, located in the Latin Quarter of Paris, had been a seminary and was run-down, dark, and damp—but blind children would not notice that. It had also been an orphanage, and Vincent de Paul, the future saint, had lived and worked there in the seventeenth century, providing comfort and relief to the poor, the stricken, and the imprisoned.

The reestablishment of an institute for the blind, managed by returned aristocrats and again graced with the designation "royal," took place in 1818. In February 1819, the ten-year-old blind son of the saddler was enrolled as the seventieth pupil. His name was Louis Braille. The director of the school was extremely frugal and very strict with his pupils; he drilled them as if they were in reform school. They did not learn much, but music was the director's hobby, and in that the boys were given free rein. Such reading lessons as they got made use of books with relief print, across which they ran their fingers until they could make out words and sentences. It was extremely slow and laborious, and did not make reading very accessible to the boys. In truth, the Royal Institute for Blind Children was little more than a workhouse with miserable accommodations and food.

Conditions improved when a gifted young doctor, André Pignier, became director. For twenty years, Pignier would battle indifference and bureaucracy to get better facilities for his pupils. He was the first to realize that sighted people could not understand what it was like not to be able to see and so were poorly equipped to lead the blind. The blind were asked to learn what the sighted learned, to read the same letters and words, but using their fingers rather than their eyes. In this they were making little progress.

Pignier made the acquaintance of an army captain named Charles Barbier, a man with an idée fixe. Barbier had devised a system in which dots and dashes were impressed on a piece of cardboard by an awl attached to a ruler. With this system, he believed, soldiers in the field could receive their orders at night by coded instructions they could sense with their fingers, rather than by light signals, which were dangerous. The raised surface of dots and dashes on the reverse side of the cardboard, when touched in the dark, gave the code. Neither the army nor scientific circles had showed any interest in Barbier's system, which he called *l'écriture nocturne*, night-writing, so he brought it to the institute to be tested.

The pupils tackled the task enthusiastically, since they had little else to do except, in good weather, to go for walks in the botanical garden, clutching a rope like the members of a chain gang. Barbier's new system proved a disappointment. It was a sort of shorthand using a phonetic script. It could be read a little faster than relief print because of the use of code, but it was no aid to learning anything because nothing had been written in that code. It could pass on limited information in the dark but was totally unsuited to the education of the blind. The inventor, however, maintained until his death that he had solved their reading problem.

Louis Braille learned to put up with his lot; he worked on simple handicrafts, played music, and absorbed what he could from the few books available to him. He was a gifted, industrious pupil who fought the limitations of his handicap. He understood that touching letters or codes had to substitute for perceiving them visually, and realized that their meaning was apprehended not in the eyes, but in the brain. An alphabet that was suitable for fingers, therefore, did not need to be the same as one designed for eyes that could see.

The skin of the fingertips contains a network of receptors that transmit to the brain the position, intensity, and sequence of a tactile stimulus. A fingertip pressure of a few grams per millimeter is enough to cause the sensation of touch. Braille knew from bitter experience that the fingering of large raised letters made hardly any use of this subtle tactile ability. With iron determination, he set about searching for a code that would. He experimented with an awl and heavy paper, producing a four-dot code that varied the number and position of the dots to represent letters. He expanded the code to six dots, arranged in three pairs, one below the other: an alphabet of domino-like patterns. Perhaps the game of dominoes, popular at that time in France and Italy, actually gave him the idea.

Many technological inventions have given rise to scientific insights. The fire-engine pump showed Harvey how the blood circulates; the internal combustion engine illustrates the physiology of the heart; and the computer is used to explore theories about the structure of the human brain. Braille writing was such an invention. At the very beginning of human evolution, the hand was essential as a tool for man the creator, homo faber. Over time, the sense of touch became less important than the hand's manipulative skill, its motor ability to work and gesture. A blind person, undistracted by the dominant sensory information that vision provides, "sees" through his hands, and by touch can conjure up a world of associations. The blind have a different and often more developed perception of their environment. They demonstrate the possibilities open to people when the power of sight fails.

Braille's six dots yielded sixty-three symbols. The dots were spaced about three millimeters apart. A century would pass before neurologists determined that the minimum distance the fingertips are capable of detecting is two millimeters. Six dots represent the maximum amount of information that one fleeting touch can absorb. A sighted person using the Braille system feels only a series of dots and has trouble interpreting them. But a blind Braille reader can take in 60 to 120 words per minute, can translate as many as 3,000 dots per minute into meaningful sentences. Usually an index finger does the reading, but a thumb, a toe, even the tip of one's nose can be used. The blind reader, just like a person with sight, perceives words, lines of text, rather than individual letters. The touch of his finger is the equivalent of the movement of a sighted person's eye: both finger and eye are in instantaneous communication with the brain for the processing of information.

Almost half a century before Braille, Denis Diderot, editor of the famous *Encyclopédie,* had become interested in deafness and blindness and had made extensive observations about them. He believed that the souls of the blind resided in their fingertips, that their thoughts originated there. Braille's invention demonstrated that eyes and fingertips were simply organs of perception, while the faculty of language resided in the brain alone. This discovery of a way to transmit information to the brain through touch gave a reader of Braille the same advantages possessed by a sighted reader. Had he not been blind, Braille could not have accomplished this; no sighted person could have had his intuition.

In 1825, Braille and his fellow students, assisted by their director, constructed a small tablet, a simple drawing board with a movable ruler that contained openings through which dots could be impressed on a thick sheet of paper. This device allowed the blind to write rapidly, in a notation that could be read by another blind person with equal speed. It gave the institute an enormous opportunity, but the financial means were lacking.

Braille, blind for fifteen years and a pupil at the institute for eight, now became a teacher in his own school. He proved to be a gifted instructor, always ready to help and completely dedicated to the education of the blind. Wanting his system to become the door to the world for those who could not see, he never stopped working on ways to improve it. It turned out that the system could also be used to notate music, and Braille became the organist of a neighborhood church.

The authorities, however, had no faith in Braille's system, and Captain Barbier claimed it was his night-writing distorted beyond recognition. Braille therefore decided to publicize his invention— in a booklet printed in outmoded relief letters. He described his system of dots in such a manner that both the blind and the sighted could understand it. At first the booklet attracted little attention. Then, after 1830, when the bourgeois king Louis Philippe took power, France revived. Visitors came to tour the institute; some of its pupils became teachers at other institutes; and the Braille system was demonstrated at exhibitions and in concerts given by blind musicians. The institute received new recognition and support. It produced a number of books using the new system—books assembled by blind boys in an old reformatory and paid for out of their own pockets. The first Braille book was a brief history of France, printed by hand on thick paper, in three volumes comprising a total of two hundred pages and weighing four and a half pounds.

Yet the bureaucrats, as well as the deputy director of the institute, believed that for the blind to have a language of their own would only drive them deeper into darkness and isolation. The answer, they thought, lay in the old relief printing, which served both those who could see and those who couldn't. Louis Braille tried to narrow the gap between the two methods, and in this he was assisted by another talented blind man, Pierre Foucault. Together they devised a mechanical typewriter with ten metal fingers that inscribed raised dots on paper. Here was a writing machine available to all the blind. Later, this machine was adapted to produce music notation as well.

In 1844, the Royal Institute for Blind Children was finally given more decent accommodations. At the opening ceremony in the new quarters, there was an elaborate demonstration of the Braille system in words and music. Braille himself was present, grateful for the recognition but aware that his days were numbered. Eight years earlier, he had started to cough up blood; he had contracted tuberculosis during his years of poverty and malnutrition in the old, damp building, and it was sapping his strength. When he felt well enough, he played the organ. Mostly he stayed in his room, wasting away. He distributed all his possessions. He told his former director that God had been good to him by permitting him to alleviate the lot of those who shared his misfortune: his blindness, he felt, had been of benefit to his soul. In January 1852, Braille died. Both the blind and the sighted came to pay their respects. A death mask was made for a monument, but the monument was never erected. Braille's body was delivered to his eldest brother and returned by horse-drawn cart to the small country village where he had been born. Family members and friends attended the funeral, and Louis Braille, beyond the confines of the institute, remained unknown.

His system would have its followers but also its detractors, because some begrudged the blind an alphabet of their own. It was not until 1878 that the countries of Europe decided to adopt the Braille system for the education of the blind. It was not adopted in America until 1912, and its worldwide use came only decades later, under the aegis of the United Nations and the World Health Organization. Today it is the universal alphabet of forty million blind people, and programming and printing technology have provided many new applications in music and science. The American Helen Keller, blind and deaf from infancy, learned to read and write with Braille, graduated from college cum laude, and devoted her life to helping the deaf and the blind. On the hundredth anniversary of Louis Braille's death, she wrote that in the Sahara of blindness he had sowed a gift of inexhaustible fertility and joy. It was thanks to him that she had gained access to the worlds of poetry, history, and literature.

Braille did not become a famous Frenchman like Pasteur or Charcot. No street or square was named after him. Because of his blindness, he was unknown and unrecognized in the land of the sighted: a minor saint, overlooked by church and state, a poor blind man with tuberculosis who had lived in an institution. The French state tried to make amends on the anniversary of his death in 1952. The saddler's cottage in which Braille grew up was restored. In the workshop hangs the tool that may have blinded him. The peace of his grave was disturbed, and his earthly remains were taken in procession to Paris to be housed in the Pantheon, that former church desecrated by the Revolution and reserved for the great of France. The honors paid to the first tenants had been inconstant. Marat, the instigator of the September massacres, was carried in triumphantly through the front entrance but removed later by the back door. Braille was given a place beside three naturalists of modest stature rather than in the company of the great writers of his time, Victor Hugo and Emile Zola.

The village of his birth, Coupvray, unhappy about losing its only famous son to Paris, complained that it was left with an empty grave. A compromise was worked out. The hands whose touch had discovered a new writing were severed and placed in a small concrete casket in the empty grave. Braille's body was moved into the basement of the Pantheon, back to oblivion.

Translated by Johan Theron

Manifest Destiny

(For Diana Michener)

1

(Pink Palace Museum, Memphis)

She lifts the bullet out of the blazing case.
Here.
   What can it harm?
Clock on the wall.
   Ceiling-fan on.
Earlier it was

muzzleflash, dust. All round in the woods
   voices and orders but you can't be sure whose.
Here's a sunken place by the road for
   shelter, for the speechless
reload.

   Tents that way or is it fog?
Or is it freedom?
   A horse with his dead man
disappears.
   The line is *where* that has to be maintained at all

cost?
   Smoke clears and here's
a thousand peachtrees,
   a massacre of blooms, or is it smoke?—

the fire is let go, travels into the blossoming (not as fast
    as you'd

think) enters a temple then a thigh.
    Carrying one body into the other.
She holds up the set of knives in their calfskin case.
    Behind her the diorama where the field surgeon's
sawing.
    There's the wax mouth held shut.
There's the scream inside—gold, round.
    Peachblossoms fall.
No chloroform so whiskey's

    used and sometimes—now lifting up out of the
incandescent case—the
    bullet we bend close
to see the
    bitemarks on—three dark impressions—whose footprints
on bottomland—
    whose 8,000 bodies, sticky with blossom, loosening into the wet field,
the still-living moving the more

    obedient bodies of the already-dead
up and down during the night,
    petals continuing to cover them.
Flashes of lightning showed hogs feeding on the dead says the
    captain who hears the wounded rebel under him say "oh
God what made You

    come down here to fight? we never
would have come up there."
    Look, he lives to write it down,

here are the black words photographed and blown
    up wall-size behind
the guide.
    Do you think these words are still enough?
And the next thing and the next thing?
    Where is the mark that stays?
Where is what makes a mark

that stays?
    What's *real* slides through.
The body rots. The body won't hold it.
    Here's the next room and the *flight simulator.*
We the living run our arms along the grooves as we walk through.
    They are lifted and dropped.
Experience wingaction.
    I shut my eyes and try it

again.
    The museum hums round me.
Something else,
    something niggardly letting the walls stay up for now, hums,
something speechless and dense and stationary letting

    matter coalesce
in obstinate illustration—hums.
    Hear the theories come to cloak it—buzz—
Hear the deafness all over the trees, green—
    Hear his scream go into the light—
See how the light is untouched
    by the scream that
enters it.
    Dust motes.
Peachblossom-fall.

Where shall the scream stick?
What shall it dent?
Won't the deafness be cracked?
Won't the molecules be loosened?

Are you listening: we need the scream to leave its mark
on the silky down of
the petalled
light.

I lift my arms along the rutted ledge.
Lift, drop, try to feel the prey beneath me.
Look down through the trees
only there is no *through* anymore it all being flat, flat, a
fabric, skin, something's deep
sleep,
then the dropping
down fast
to try to scratch

the emptiness—"I was there, *I was there*" or
"It was a most beautiful evening" Private Leander Stilwell of the
100th Indiana remembered. "It really seemed like Sunday in the country
at home."

2
(Peach Orchard, Shiloh Battlefield)
(Mississippi River)

She's the scream he's the light.
They are playing, sort of, at Leda and Swan.

No, she's the *stream* he's the *blossomfall?*

Do you think these words are still enough?

Something out there on a spot in the middle of the
river

where the sun hits first and most directly

where a person can hardly look

where there's a little gash on the waterfilm

an indentation almost a cut his foothold

a *taking* there, though not slowly like rot,

a *likeness* there, a subtraction,

a dizziness rushing down
into thought—

her a stream, yes, though not less a
girl; and him the light become winged in its lower
reaches, almost biting the water there where it touches

or so the story goes

him needing something he did not have

filtering down to make the silt-life glow,
down onto the one-way motion, the hard
muscle of the no-turning-back—

All round them the confused clickings of matter

Somewhere behind them
a human voice calling out a time of day like a
plea

and the insects whining high and low, buzz and click, without
cessation—

So he hurts her a little, hurts her some more

Can't seem to find her, maybe he'll cut her

Can't seem to find her: can't seem to find her

The more he enters the more she disappears

The more she takes him the more he isn't true

Maybe now they will feel their bodies? (Harder)

Now do they feel them? (Harder?)

What is it to always be within oneself,
interminable noon,

watching for the face to look this way, the face

even then already bored, its glance passing
over—

Is it death they want to touch, or is it invent—

Their difference a kindling in the endlessness—

Is that what they wanted—to make a beginning, to introduce
ruin, an aperture that lets in the minutes, the buzzing and then
the festering—

Oh the minutes can't you hear them already behind this blossoming
white page

greedy awaiting the fresh wound

black wings beating, antennae wild, sticky and thousand-eyed,
sacks of their blood beneath their wings—

He wants to go into her, he goes through

The toothed light down hard on the sinewy scream

He ties her down with his belt she is not there

She is asking for it he is not there

He promises forever she is not there

Do I own you she says

yes, yes he is not there

She is rising up as he descends then she
    is not
there then she
    is water beneath him, a river is flowing

He's clawing for foothold the river won't take his mark—

What can he seize?

Where she eddies it's brighter for an instant—
Where the scream is, the light is broken for
                    the instant—
Where the light is brighter the scream is
                    the instant—
Where they thought they could marry—
In which they thought they could touch
                    each other—
The instant: they can't see it: a scent: in it
        the place something maybe took

place but what—

Perhaps it is a hate they want to feel, a pure one without
cause

like a *lateness* outside the sensation of time

like a sunlight beating down or a loud voice utterly without
syllables

him the center of a what-will-I-be, what-shall-I-
think-about

with a laundry list and a nobility and a question to ask her when
he finally gets his hands on her

the whole damn thing here sucking and buzzing like a silver
wrapper he's supposed to get off

Oh but get up get up the world is strange there is no
                        underneath

get up, the light is blossoming *like foil* but also it itches and is an
iceberg

and now raises its head (like a swan like a sunlight)

and now raises its head wanting to be alive

How can the scream rise up out of its grave of matter
How can the light drop down out of its grave of thought

How can they cross over and the difference between them swell with
existence

Everything at the edges of everything else now rubbing

making tiny sounds that add up into laughter

something the breeze can lift and drop

something that clots here and there and confirms our
fear

(and the laughter which you might *think* is an angel
above them)

(a body whose ribs are the limits of everything)

(oh but we are *growing* now that there's a hurry, aren't we?)

(here where nothing is alive and vastly-limbed and -eyed)

(and the future spreads before us the back of its long
                                        body)

For the first time since Homer . . . whispers his open book,
spine up to the light

and *Naturalism was already outmoded when* . . .

and *by visible truth we mean the apprehension of* . . .

3

Beautiful natural blossoms,
    little mist of broken starlight,
what is this she lifts and puts into my hand,
    this leaden permanence
punched through with pain—ash

    of a man's scream still
intact?
    Strange how heavy it is I think.
And here are the in-

    dentations—
I run my finger in them,
    little consequence, darker than the cause.

    The war is gone. The reason gone. The body gone. Its
reason gone. The name the face the personal
    identity and yet here
is a pain that will not
    diminish—
What do we call it when, pain gone, the

force of the pain is still un-
    wavering—
knife sawing the leg, bone breaking, the opening of
    the slice, cold air
where flesh had been—
    What do we call it,

the air round this gray
    fossil of pure
carnal
    limit.
Is it free?

    I stand with my hand out in front of me.
The others look into it. Someone puts his fingers in,
    lifts it slightly, then puts it back down
on my warm palm.
    Already it is less cold than it was.
Already some of the heat has entered its molecule.
    Already our words and the tone of our words, the ex-

    clamation mark, the rising supplication of
the question mark have mixed into the high-ceilinged museum
    air.
Some of the heat from our bodies has crossed out
    on the back of the words.
Some small attribute, some gaseous

    nature of the
thing has changed,
    hasn't it?
I'm looking for contagion. I'm watching the face

of my friend as he tries to see
deeply the bitten bullet without
    lifting his hand to touch.
I watch his eyes focus.
    I watch him try to see what there is to

see.
    The russet cord behind him gleams.
The ceiling fan.
    The woman's voice.
The window to the
    left and through it

    blossoms in rain.
Little mist,
    you take the sunlight and its frequency,
which is a color, in,
    you have these teeth which are molecules,
and in them there is
    a form of desire

which ascertains what color of the light
    will do, into which then the molecules must bite
down, taking the necessary
    nutrient—color? speed?—
into themselves and,
    altering, matter

make—white and silky by virtue of what they
    do not
apprehend—

What does this young man's bite into the world

take—
what nutrient
    does his bite find,

    what grows, white and airy and almost invisible,
out of him
    as of this
feeding?
    What has he swallowed that will now root and rise
up through him and blossom
    up through his back, out through the eyes, the sockets, pits,
out the hole at the end of each fingertip—?

Here is the young man's great-grandfather himself a young
                            man who gets off the boat
    in James Town, 1754, with a sack of
seeds. This is a peach seed. It has come from
    Amsterdam. Before it was in a crate
unloaded in Venice.
    A new thing for the human mind—a peach—found
in Baghdad by another young man and tasted out of
    curiosity. The pit is collected. An interesting
fruit part apple part pear he writes in his travelogue.
    Here is the spring of 1762 and the first blossoms,
and then a good summer, not much war, and then the first
    fruit.
Here is the wife's face, he is handing her a fruit.
    She puts the churn down a minute. The child is
crying in the basket by the fire.
    Here, he says, try it. And her mouth
over the rough skin.
    The fire needing attention. The child

starting to scream.

    Here is the mark on the surface of that

peach.

    Here the note she puts in her journal that night.

The words for it—that taste.

    The season it stands at the heart of, that

sweetness not entirely sweet.

    A fruit part sunshine part water she writes.

But what she's thinking is his face when he came into the room

    holding it

this morning. What was it he held in his hand

    that his face

could not see,

    could not hold?

Arc

Joan turns her armored chest toward you.
She says:

I was burning
when they came for me to burn me.

Her breastplate gathers to a point, it points
at her chin.

How controlled, how symmetrical she is
in a mildewed bedroom over crooked streets.

No, there is a collision, there is hair and sweat,
she is in disorder, she has not yet said:

If a flower comes it reflects a flower,
if a bird comes it reflects a bird.

She is still plastic,
her feet bleed

as they drag her over the oval stones,
each with its oval shine.

She is still a mess, the it has not dressed her
for the hole yet, in Christ on his globe

and golden lilies on a white satin field.

I Am the Elder

I am the elder
who gets superseded

by a gold cross on a hillside,
the blue sea divided.

I ate the red seeds and the pits.
I could wear a necklace for protection,

turn my body into a city-state
or a delicate and varied landscape

greedy for attention.
Some weeds wave silver paws in the sun.

Why is the long hair caught in his lips,
why is her pallor romantic?

Why is someone sturdy not marching
across the square to save us?

Fountain

(After Duchamp: 1–6)

◆

La Fortune

(After Man Ray: 1–6)

Fountain (After Duchamp: 1), 1991

La Fortune (After Man Ray: 1), 1990

Fountain (After Duchamp: 2), 1991

La Fortune (After Man Ray: 2), 1990

Fountain (After Duchamp: 3), 1991

La Fortune (After Man Ray: 3), 1990

Fountain (After Duchamp: 4), 1991

La Fortune (After Man Ray: 4), 1990

Fountain (After Duchamp: 5), 1991

La Fortune (After Man Ray: 5), 1990

Fountain (After Duchamp: 6), 1991

La Fortune (After Man Ray: 6), 1990

Fountain (After Duchamp: 1–6)
La Fortune (After Man Ray: 1–6)

S herrie Levine emerged in the late 1970s at a moment characterized by a reevaluation of representational art and the nature of the art object itself. In the wake of minimalism and conceptual art, Levine and others wanted to consider the meaning of art for a generation that had grown up surrounded by photographic reproductions and by television. Of particular ideological importance was the recognition that the mass media were a primary force shaping late-twentieth-century culture.

In her series *After Walker Evans* (1981), Levine copied ("rephotographed") such well-known images as Evans's depression farmers, creating works that were virtually indistinguishable from Evans's originals. This radically reductive gesture brought under fire received notions of the relative value of originals and copies. Levine argued that reproductions of fine art masterpieces were no less products of mass culture than the images of Elvis or Liz Taylor appropriated and reproduced by Andy Warhol. This linking of the rarefied art object to the mass-produced one is a legacy not only of pop art and the repeated "serial" forms of minimalism but, ultimately, of the readymades of Marcel Duchamp. These seemingly ordinary objects recontextualized as art were unquestionably the first works consciously to challenge the once rigidly maintained divide between art and mass production, between high and low culture. Through these works, Duchamp insisted on the primacy of conceptual strategies over plastic concerns, and the consequences reverberate today.

Levine's debt to Duchamp has been considerable, as can be seen both in her copying of the drawings of Malevich and Schiele and in her reducing the history of abstraction to generic stripes and checkerboards. The irony of claiming modern masters as postmodern readymades becomes all the more acute when Levine recognizes Duchamp's own historical status and appropriates the work of the first appropriator. In her 1991 series *Fountain (After Duchamp)*, Levine confronts Duchamp head-on by replicating his most controversial readymade. Duchamp, under a pseudonym, entered his *Fountain* (1917) for the first exhibition of the American Society of Independent Artists; it was an ordinary porcelain urinal, signed "R. Mutt." Its rejection from that show is testimony to how far it stretched the limits of art practice. For Levine, however, *Fountain* is emblematic. The historical significance of its radical challenge has entered it in the canon—as attested by its constant reproduction in art texts—and, paradoxically, rendered it precious. Levine has accordingly rendered her *Fountain (After Duchamp)* in polished bronze, transforming it into a gleaming objet d'art.

For this portfolio, Levine has thrown the readymade status of reproduced art into sharp focus by presenting the entire edition of *Fountain (After Duchamp: 1–6)*. Also included is the entire edition of another work, *La Fortune (After Man Ray: 1–6)* (1990), a series of functional, three-dimensional replicas of a billiard table pictured in Man Ray's dreamy, surrealist landscape of 1938.

This portfolio itself is both an homage and a critique of the idea of homage. By juxtaposing Duchamp and Man Ray, Levine recalls that they are historically linked as the essential conspirators of New York Dada from 1915 onward. At the same time, Levine understands that the integrity of authorship is constantly assailed by the mass dissemination of imagery. In coupling and repeating these images by Duchamp and Man Ray, she acknowledges both their influence and the forces undermining the claims made for their mastery.

—Howard Halle

To Kill a Child

I t's a peaceful day as sunlight settles onto the fields of the plain. Soon bells will be ringing, because today is Sunday. Between fields of rye, two children have just come upon a footpath that they have never taken before, and in the three villages along the plain, windowpanes glisten in the sun. Men shave before mirrors propped on kitchen tables, women hum as they slice up cinnamon bread for the morning meal, and children sit on kitchen floors, buttoning the fronts of their shirts. This is the pleasant morning of an evil day, because on this day a child will be killed in the third village by a cheerful man. Yet the child still sits on the kitchen floor, buttoning his shirt. And the man who is still shaving talks of the day ahead, of their rowing trip down the creek. And still humming, the woman places the freshly cut bread on a blue plate.

No shadows pass over the kitchen, and yet even now the man who will kill the child stands near a red gas pump in the first village. He's a cheerful man, looking through the viewfinder of his camera, framing a shot of a small blue car and a young woman who stands beside it, laughing. As the woman laughs and the man snaps the charming picture, the attendant screws their gas cap on tightly. He tells them it looks like a good day for a drive. The woman gets into the car, and the man who will kill the child pulls out his wallet. He tells the attendant they're driving to the sea. He says when they reach the sea they'll rent a boat and row far, far out. Through her open window, the woman in the front seat hears his words. She settles back and closes her eyes. And with her eyes closed she sees the sea and the man sitting beside her in a boat. He's not an evil man, he's carefree and cheerful. Before he climbs into the car, he stands for a moment in front of the grille, which gleams in the sun, and he enjoys the mixed aroma of gasoline and lilacs. No shadows fall over the car, and its shiny bumper has no dents, nor is it red with blood.

But just as the man in the first village climbs into his car and slams the door shut, and as he is reaching down to pull out the choke, the woman in the third village opens her kitchen cupboard and finds that she has no sugar. The child, who has finished buttoning his shirt and has tied his shoes, kneels on a couch and sees the stream winding between the alders, pictures the black rowboat pulled up into the tall grass of the bank. The man who will lose his child has finished shaving and is just now closing his portable mirror. Coffee cups, cinnamon bread, cream, and flies each have a place on the table. Only the sugar is missing. And so the mother tells her child to run over to the Larssons' to borrow a little. As the child opens the door, the man calls after him, urging him to hurry, because the boat lies waiting for them on the bank of the creek, and today they will row much, much further than they ever have before. Running through the yard, the child can think of nothing else but the stream and the boat and the fish that jump from the water. And no one whispers to the child that he has only eight minutes to live and that the boat will lie where it is today and for many days to come.

It isn't far to the Larssons'. It's only across the road. And just as the child is crossing that road, the small blue car is speeding through the second village. It's a tiny village, with humble red houses and newly awakened people who sit in their kitchens with raised coffee cups. They look out over their hedges and see the car rush past, a large cloud of dust rising behind it. The car moves fast, and from behind the steering wheel, the man catches glimpses of apple trees and newly tarred telephone poles slipping past like gray shadows. Summer breathes through their open windows, and as they rush out of the second village their car hugs the road, riding safely, surely, in the middle. They are alone on this road—

so far. It's a peaceful thing, to drive completely alone on a broad road. And as they move out onto the open plain, that feeling of peace settles deeper. The man is strong and contented, and with his right elbow he can feel the woman's body. He's not a bad man. He's in a hurry to get to the sea. He wouldn't hurt even the simplest creature, and yet, still, he will soon kill a child. As they rush on toward the third village, the woman again shuts her eyes, pretending those eyes will not open again until they can look on the sea. In time with the car's gentle swaying, she dreams about the calm, lapping tide, the peaceful, mirrored surface of the sea.

Because life is constructed in such a merciless fashion, even one minute before a cheerful man kills a child he can still feel entirely at ease, and only one minute before a woman screams out in horror she can close her eyes and dream of the sea, and during the last minute of that child's life his parents can sit in a kitchen waiting for sugar, talking casually about the child's white teeth and the rowing trip they have planned, and that child himself can close a gate and begin to cross a road, holding in his right hand a few cubes of sugar wrapped up in white paper, and for the whole of that minute he can see nothing but a clear stream with big fish and a wide-bottomed boat with silent oars.

Afterward, everything is too late. Afterward, there is a blue car stopped sideways in the road, and a screaming woman takes her hand from her mouth, and it's dark with blood. Afterward, a man opens a car door and tries to stand on his legs, even though he has a pit of horror within him. Afterward, a few sugar cubes are strewn meaninglessly about in the blood and gravel, and a child lies motionless on its stomach, its face pressed heavily against the road. Afterward, two pale people, who have not yet had their coffee, come running through a gate to see a sight in the road they will never forget. Because it's not true that time heals all wounds. Time does not heal the wounds of a killed child, and it heals very poorly the pain of a mother who forgot to buy sugar and who sent her child across the road to borrow some. And it heals just as poorly the anguish of a once-cheerful man who has killed a child.

Because the man who has killed a child does not go to the sea. The man who has killed a child drives home slowly, in silence. And beside him sits a mute woman with a bandaged hand. And as they drive back through the villages, they do not see even one friendly face—all shadows, everywhere, are very dark. And when they part, it is in the deepest silence. And the man who has killed a child knows that this silence is his enemy, and that he will need years of his life to conquer it by crying out that it wasn't his fault. But he also knows that this is a lie. And in the fitful dreams of his nights he will try instead to gain back just a single minute of his life, to somehow make that single minute different.

But life is so merciless to the man who has killed a child that everything afterward is too late.

Translated by Steven Hartman, with Lo Dagerman

Moth Moon

A man who has worn away his hair
against the pillow by shaking
his head
No.

The man who stands over him
whispering secrets of poisonous snow.

A woman who suffers from Dutch elm disease,
who speaks to her hands
as they turn to dried leaves
falling
outside the window—
her hands covering the ground.

The porch light snaps on.
The man
who had wandered away now appears:
smoking his cigarette,
watching.

The insects gather. The moths
have finally found their moon.
Here on earth, wings burning.
Bodies falling slowly, like ashes
they had hoped they would rise from.

Three Protrusions

Where was the woman who said she'd come. She said she would come. He thought she'd have come by now. He sat and thought. He was in the living room. When he started waiting one window was full of yellow light across the floor and he was still waiting as that shadow began to fade and was intersected by a brightening shadow from a different wall's window. There was an insect on one of the steel shelves that held his audio equipment. The insect kept going in and out of one of the holes on the girders that the shelves fit into. The insect was dark and had a shiny case. He kept looking over at it. Once or twice he started to get up to go over closer to look at it, but he was afraid that if he came closer and saw it closer he would kill it, and he was afraid to kill it. He did not use the phone to call the woman who'd promised to come because if he tied up the line and if it happened to be the time when maybe she was trying to call him he was afraid she would hear the busy signal and think him disinterested and get angry and maybe take what she'd promised him somewhere else.

She had promised to get him a quarter of a pound of marijuana, four ounces of unusually good marijuana, for $550. He had tried to stop smoking marijuana maybe seventy or eighty times before. Before this woman knew him. She did not know he had tried to stop. He always lasted a week, or two weeks, or maybe two days, and then he'd think and decide to have some in his home one more last time. One last final time he'd search out someone new, someone he hadn't already told that he had to stop smoking dope and please under no circumstances should they procure him any dope. It had to be a third party, because he'd told every dealer he knew to cut him off. And the third party had to be someone new, because each time he got some he knew this time had to be the last time, and so told them, asked them, as a favor, never to get him any more, ever. And he never asked a person again once he'd told them this, because he was proud, and also kind, and wouldn't put anyone in that kind of contradictory position. Also he considered himself creepy when it came to dope, and he was afraid that others would see that he was creepy about it as well. He sat and thought and waited in an uneven X of light through two different windows. Once or twice he looked at the phone. The insect had disappeared back into the hole in the steel girder a shelf fit into.

She'd promised to come at one certain time, and it was past that time. Finally he called and it rang and he was afraid of how much time he was taking tying up the line and he got her answering machine, the message had a snatch of radio music and her voice and a male voice saying we'll call you back, and the "we" made them sound like a couple, the man was a handsome black man who was in law school, she designed sets, and he didn't leave a message because he didn't want her to know how much now he felt like he needed it. He had been very casual about the whole thing. She said she knew a guy over in Enfield who sold high-resin dope in moderate bulk, and he'd yawned and said well, maybe, well, hey, why not, sure, special occasion, I haven't bought any in I don't know how long. He said he guessed he'd have her get a decent amount, he said he'd had some friends call him in the recent past and ask if he could get them some. He had this thing where he'd frequently say he was getting dope for friends. Then if the woman didn't have it when she said she'd have it for him and he became anxious about it he could tell the woman that it was his friends who were becoming anxious, and he was sorry to bother the woman about something so casual but his friends were anxious and bothering him about it and he just wanted to know what he could tell them. He was caught in the middle, is

how he would represent it. He could say his friends had given
him their money and were now anxious and exerting pressure.
This tactic was not possible with this woman who'd said she'd
come because he hadn't yet given her the $550. She would not
let him. She was well off. Her family was well off, she'd said to
explain how her condominium was how it was when she worked
designing sets for a Cambridge theater company that seemed to do
only German plays, dark smeary sets. She didn't care much about
money, she said she'd cover the cost when she got out to Enfield
to see whether the guy was at home as she was certain he would be
this particular afternoon, and he could pay her back when she got
it. This arrangement, very casual, made him anxious, so he'd been
even more casual and said sure, fine, whatever. Thinking back, he
was sure he'd said "whatever," which in retrospect worried him
because it might have sounded like he didn't care at all, not at
all, so little that it wouldn't matter if she forgot to get it or call,
and once he'd made the decision to have marijuana in his home
one more time it mattered a lot. It mattered a lot. He'd been too
casual, he should have made her take $550 from him up front,
claiming politeness, claiming he didn't want to inconvenience her
financially over something so trivial and casual. He didn't care
much about money either, money was not where his greed lay. He
had his share of the emotion of greed, but somehow it wasn't for
money. But money did create a sense of obligation, and he did
want the woman to feel obliged to do what she'd said once what
she'd said she'd do had set him off inside. It mattered so much
somehow he was afraid to show how much it mattered. Once he
had asked her to get it, he was committed to several courses of
action. The insect on the shelf was back. It didn't seem to do
anything. It just came out of the hole in the girder onto the edge
of the steel shelf and sat there. After a while it would disappear
back into the hole in the girder, and he was pretty sure it didn't
do anything in there either. He felt similar to the insect inside the
girder his shelf was connected to but was not sure just how he was
similar. Once he'd decided to own marijuana one more last time,
he was committed to several courses of action. He had to call in to
the agency and say there was an emergency and ask them to put a
note in a colleague's box asking her to cover his calls for the rest of
the week because he'd be out of town for several days due to this

emergency. He had to put a message on his answering machine
saying that starting that afternoon he was going to be unreachable
for several days. He had to clean his bedroom, because once he
had dope he would not leave his bedroom except to go to the
refrigerator and the bathroom, and even then the trips would be
very quick. He had to throw out all his beer and liquor, because if
he drank alcohol and smoked dope at the same time he would get
dizzy and ill, and if he had alcohol in the house he could not be
relied on not to drink it once he started smoking dope. He had
to do some shopping. He had to lay in supplies. Now just one of
the insect's antennae was protruding from the hole in the girder.
It protruded but did not move. Somehow he formed the analogy
that when he had committed himself to one last vacation with
marijuana, but the marijuana had not yet arrived, something in
him protruded but did not move. He spent several hundred clicks
of the portable clock next to the telephone on this analogy, not
extending the analogy or trying to analyze it, but simply letting
it sit there. He had had to buy soda, Oreos, bread, sandwich
meat, mayonnaise, tomatoes, M&M's, Almost Home cookies, ice
cream, a Pepperidge Farm frozen chocolate cake, and four cans
of canned chocolate frosting to be eaten with a large spoon. He'd
had to rent film cartridges from the entertainment service. He'd
had to buy antacids for the discomfort that eating all he would
eat would cause late at night. He'd had to buy a bong, because
each time he finished what had to be his last bulk-quantity of
marijuana he decided that that was it, he was through, he didn't
even like it anymore, that was it, no more hiding, no more putting
different messages on his answering machine and moving his car
away from his condominium and closing his windows and curtains
and blinds and living in vectors between his television and VCR
and his refrigerator and his toilet, and he would throw the bong
away wrapped in numerous paper bags. His refrigerator made its
own ice in little cloudy crescent blocks and he loved it, when he
had dope in his home he always drank a great deal of cold soda
and ice water. His tongue almost swelled at the thought. He looked
at the phone and the clock. He looked at the windows but not at
the foliage and driveway beyond the windows. He had already
vacuumed his venetian blinds and curtains, everything was ready
to be shut down. Once the woman who'd said she'd come had

come, he would shut the system down. It occurred to him that he would disappear into a hole in a girder inside him that supported something else inside him. He was unsure what the thing inside him was and was unprepared to commit himself to the course of action that would be required to explore the question. It was now almost three hours past the time when the woman had said she would come. A counselor, Randi, with an *i*, with a mustache like a Mountie, had said in the outpatient treatment program he'd gone through two years ago that he seemed insufficiently committed to the course of action that would be required to remove substances from his life. He'd had to buy a new bong at Bogarts in Cambridge because whenever he finished the last of the substances on hand he always threw out his bong and pipes, screens and tubes and rolling papers and roach clips, lighters and Visine and Pepto-Bismol and cookies and cakes, to eliminate all temptation. He wrapped everything in Star Market shopping bags and drove it out to some dumpster in some disreputable location, and discarded it. He removed all dope-related materials from his life each time. He always felt a great relief and optimism after he'd discarded the materials. He'd bought the new bong and laid in supplies this morning, getting back home with everything well before the woman had said she'd come. He thought of the new bong and new little packet of brass screens in the Bogarts bag on his kitchen table in the sunlit kitchen and could not remember what color this new bong was. The last one had been orange, the one before that a dusky rose color that had turned muddy at the bottom from resin in just four days. He could not remember the color of this new last bong. He considered getting up to check the color of the bong he'd be using but decided that obsessive checking and convulsive movements could compromise the atmosphere of casual calm he needed to maintain while he waited, protruding but not moving, for the woman he'd met at a design session for his agency's small campaign for her small theater company's new Brecht festival, while he waited for this woman, with whom he'd had intercourse twice, to honor her casual promise. He tried to decide whether she was pretty. Another thing he laid in when he'd committed himself to one last marijuana vacation was petroleum jelly. When he smoked marijuana he tended to masturbate a great deal, and the petroleum jelly kept him from returning to normal function all sore. He was also hesitant to get up and check the color of his bong because he would have to pass right by the phone to get to the kitchen, and he didn't want to be tempted to call the woman who'd said she would come again because he felt creepy about bothering her about something so casual, and was afraid that several hang-ups on her answering machine would look even creepier, and also he felt anxious about tying up the line when she called, as she certainly would. He decided to get Call Waiting added to his phone service for a nominal extra charge, then remembered that since this was positively the last time he would or even could indulge what Randi, with an *i*, had called an addiction every bit as destructive as pure alcoholism, there would be no real need for Call Waiting, since a situation like the present one could never arise again. This line of thinking almost caused him to become angry. To ensure the composure with which he sat waiting in light in his chair he focused his senses on his surroundings. No part of the insect he'd seen was now visible. The clicks of his portable clock were really composed of three smaller clicks, signifying he supposed preparation, movement, and readjustment. His left thumbnail was noticeably longer than his right thumbnail, which was puzzling, since he clipped all his nails at the same time and never bit his nails. His necktie had bunched into a small arc between the top of his vest and the collar of his shirt. He began to grow disgusted with himself for waiting so anxiously for something that had stopped being fun anyway. He didn't even know why he liked it anymore. It made his mouth dry and his eyes dry and red and his face sag, and he hated it when his face sagged, it was as if all the integrity of all the muscles in his face was destroyed by marijuana, and he got terribly self-conscious about the fact that his face was sagging, and had long ago forbidden himself to smoke dope around anyone else. And the dope gave him a painful case of pleurisy if he smoked it for more than two straight days of heavy continuous smoking in his bedroom. It made his thoughts jut out crazily in jagged directions and made him stare like a rapt child at anything convulsive or bright—he favored video cartridges in which a lot of things blew up and there was little dialogue when he laid in video cartridges for a vacation with marijuana. He gathered his intellect, will, self-knowledge, and conviction and determined that when this woman came as she surely would this would simply be his last marijuana debauch. He'd simply smoke so much so fast that it would be so unpleasant and the memory of it so repulsive that once he'd gotten it out of his home and his life as quickly as possible he'd never even want to do it again. He would create a really bad association with the stuff. The dope scared him. It made him afraid. It wasn't that he was afraid of it, it was that it made him afraid of everything else. He would smoke the whole quarter-pound in four days, an ounce a day, all in tight heavy economical one-hitters off a bong, an incredible, insane amount per day, he'd treat it like a penance, he'd smoke one ounce per day, starting right when he woke up and detached his tongue from the roof of his mouth and took an antacid, two or three hundred bong hits per day, an insane, unpleasant, brain-damaging amount, even though if it was good after the first ten hits he wouldn't want any more until he wanted more. He would smoke it even if he did not want it. He would use discipline and persistence and make the whole experience so unpleasant, so debased and degrading and painful, that his behavior would be henceforth modified, he'd never even want to do it again, the memory of the debauched four days to come would be so firmly, terribly emblazoned in his memory. He'd cure himself by excess. He predicted that the woman, when she came, might want to smoke some of the four ounces with him, hang out, hole up, listen to some of his impressive collection of Tito Puente recordings, and probably have intercourse. He had never once had intercourse on marijuana. The idea frankly repelled him. Two dry mouths bumping at each other, trying to kiss. His thoughts jutting and twisting around on themselves like a snake on a stick while he snorted and grimaced above her, his face sagging so that its loose folds maybe touched, limply, the folds of her loose face as it went back and forth spread out over his pillowcase. He decided he'd have her toss him what she'd promised and then would toss the $550 in large bills back at her from a distance and tell her not to let the door hit her on the bottom on the way out. He'd say "ass" instead of "bottom." He'd be so rude to her that the memory of his lack of courtesy and of her tight offended face would be a further disincentive ever, in the future, to risk calling her and repeating the course of action he had committed himself to.

He had never been so anxious for the arrival of a woman he did not want to see. He remembered clearly the last woman he'd involved in his trying just one more vacation with dope and drawn blinds. The last woman had been something called an appropriation artist, which meant she copied and embellished other art, then sold it. She had an artistic manifesto that involved radical feminist themes. He'd let her give him one of her smaller paintings, which covered half the wall over his bed and was of a famous film actress whose name he had a hard time recalling and a less famous film actor, the two of them in a scene from a well-known film, a romantic scene, an embrace, copied from a film magazine and much enlarged and made stilted, with obscenities scrawled all over it in bright brave red letters. The last woman had been sexy but not pretty, as the woman he now didn't want to see but was waiting for was pretty in a tight tanned withered Cambridge way that made her seem pretty but not sexy. The appropriation artist had been led to believe that he was a recovering speed addict, intravenous addiction to methamphetamine hydrochloride is what he remembered telling that one, he had even described the terrible taste of hydrochloride in the addict's mouth immediately after injection, he had researched the subject carefully. She had been further led to believe that marijuana kept him from using the drug with which he really had a problem, and so that if he seemed anxious to get some once she'd offered to get him some it was only because he was heroically holding out against much darker deeper more addictive urges, and he needed her to help him. He couldn't quite remember when or how she'd been given all these impressions. He had not sat down and outright bold-faced lied to her, it had been more of an impression he'd nurtured and allowed to gather its own life and force. The insect was now entirely visible. It was on the shelf that held his amplifier and equalizer. The insect might never actually have gone back into the hole in the shelf's girder. The girder protruded from the wall and was a triangle of dull silver metal with holes for shelves to fit into. The shelves that held his audio equipment were metal painted a dark industrial green and were originally made for holding canned goods. They were designed to be extra kitchen shelves. The insect sat with an immobility that seemed like the gathering of a force, it sat like the hull of a vehicle from which the engine had been for the moment removed. It was dark and had a shiny case and antennae that did not move. He had to use the bathroom. His last piece of contact from the appropriation artist, with whom he had had intercourse, and who during intercourse had sprayed perfume into the air from a mister she held in her left hand as she lay beneath him making a wide variety of sounds and spraying perfume into the air, so that he felt the cold mist of it settling on his back and shoulders and was terribly chilled, his last piece of contact after he'd disappeared with the marijuana she had gotten for him had been a card that was a pastiche photo of a doormat of rough false plastic grass with WELCOME on it and next to it a flattering publicity photo of her from her Back Bay gallery, and between them an unequal sign, an equal sign with a diagonal slash through it, and an obscenity he had assumed was directed at him scrawled in red grease pencil at the top and bottom. She had been offended because he had seen her every day for ten days, then when she'd obtained two ounces of marijuana for him he had said that she had saved his life and he was grateful and the friends to whom he'd promised to give some were grateful and she had to go right now because he had an appointment and had to leave, but that he would doubtless call her that day, and they had shared a moist kiss, and she had said she could feel his heart pounding right through his suit coat, and she had driven away in her unmuffled car, and he had gone and moved his own car to a garage several blocks away, and had walked back and drawn the blinds and curtains, and changed the message on his answering machine to one that described an emergency departure from town, and had drawn and locked his vacuumed bedroom blinds, and had taken the new rose-colored bong out of its Bogarts bag, and was not seen for three days, and ignored over a dozen messages from the appropriation artist on his answering machine expressing concern over the emergency, and had never contacted her again. He had assumed she would assume he had succumbed again to methamphetamine hydrochloride and was sparing her the agony of his descent into the hell of addiction. What it really was was that he had again decided those two ounces of reasonably good marijuana represented his final debauch with dope and that he had to cut himself off from all possible future sources of temptation and supply, and that surely included the appropriation artist. His shame at what she might perceive as his slimy conduct toward her made it easier for him to avoid her, too. Though not shame, really. More like being very uncomfortable. He had had to launder his bedding twice to get the smell of the perfume out. He went into the bathroom to use the bathroom, making it a point to look at neither the insect that sat still on the shelf to his left nor the telephone and answering machine on the small stand to his right. He was committed to touching neither. Where was the woman who had said she'd come. The new bong in the bag was a rich green that paled when the device was held up to the late-afternoon light of the window over the kitchen sink. The metal of his new stem and bowl was rough silver, with a grain, unpretty and all business. The bong was two feet tall and had a weighted base and its plastic was thick and its carb had been raggedly cut so that some rough shards of plastic protruded from the little hole and might hurt his thumb, which he decided to consider just part of the penance he would undertake after the woman had come. He left the door to the bathroom open so that he would be sure to hear the phone when it rang or the buzzer to the front door of his condominium when it sounded. In the bathroom he wept hard for only two or three seconds before the weeping stopped abruptly and he could not get it to start again. It was now over four hours since the time the woman had casually committed to come. Was he in the bathroom or in his chair near the window and near his telephone and answering machine and the insect and the window that had admitted a straight spilled bar of light when he began to wait. The light through this window was coming at an angle more and more oblique, its shadow had become a parallelogram. The light through the west window was straight and reddening. He had thought he needed to use the bathroom but was unable to. He tried putting a whole stack of video cartridges into the VCR and turning on the large television in his bedroom. He could see the bold-colored piece of appropriation art in the mirror above the television. He lowered the volume all the way and pointed the remote control device at the television like some sort of weapon. He sat on the edge of his box spring and mattress with his elbows on his knees and scanned the stack of cartridges. Each dropped and began to spin in the machine with an insectlike click and whir, and he scanned it. He was unable to distract himself with the VCR because he was unable to stay with any one entertainment cartridge for more than a few seconds. The moment he recognized what was on one cartridge he had a strong unpleasant feeling that there was something better on another cartridge and that he was missing it. He scanned for some time. The bedroom was dim because the curtains over the big window that overlooked the street had been vacuumed and pulled shut tight, so it was difficult to gauge how long he scanned. The phone rang during this interval of scanning. He was moving back out toward it before the first ring was completed, flooded with excitement, or relief, the remote control device still in his hand, but it was only a friend, calling, and when he heard that it was not the woman who had promised to bring what he'd committed the next several days to banishing from his life forever, he was shocked with disappointment, with a great deal of mistaken adrenaline shining and ringing in his system, and he got off the line with the friend to clear the line and keep it available so fast that he was sure his friend perceived him as either angry with him or just plain rude. He was further upset because his answering the phone this late in the afternoon did not jibe with the emergency message that would be on his answering machine if the friend called back after the woman had come and he'd shut the system down, and he was standing by the phone machine trying to decide whether the risk of the friend calling back was sufficient to justify changing the message on the answering machine to describe an emergency departure starting this evening instead of this afternoon, but he decided he felt that since the woman had committed to coming some time ago, his leaving the message intact would be a gesture of fidelity to her commitment, and might somehow in some oblique way strengthen that commitment. He returned to his chair. The television and VCR were still on in his bedroom and he could see through the angle of the doorway the lights from the television screen blink and shift from one primary color to another in the dim room, and for a while he killed time casually by trying to imagine what scenes on the unwatched screen the changing colors and intensities might be depicting. Reading while waiting for marijuana was out of the question. He considered masturbating but did not. He didn't reject the idea so much as not react to it and watch as it floated away. He thought very broadly of desires and ideas being watched but not acted upon, he thought of impulses being starved of expression and drying out and floating drily away, and felt on some level that this had something to do with him and his circumstances and what, if the last debauch he'd committed himself to didn't perhaps resolve the problem, would surely have to be called his problem, but he could not even begin to try to see how the image of desiccated impulses floating related to either him or the insect that was back in its hole in the girder, because at this precise time the telephone and the buzzer to the door downstairs both sounded at once, both loud and tortured and so abrupt they sounded yanked through a very small hole into the great balloon of silence he sat in, waiting, and he moved first toward the telephone, and then toward his intercom module, and then tried to move back to the phone, and then tried to move toward both at once, so that he stood splay-legged, arms wildly out as if something had been flung, splayed, entombed between the two signals, without a thought in his head.

ALAN SOLDOFSKY

The Beginning of Summer

A brightness in the skies even after dark.
A remnant sun splotch. Backlit turquoise
deepening to indigo, then black.
Lavender afterglow of clouds over Mission Peak.
The wind's delicate sharpness on my neck,
as if dusk were a saturation of lyricism.
Intolerable beauty, heartbreaking by definition,
and we are relieved by its passing.
I am appalled by the sensation of being
governed by the body. Swallowing, yawning, having to pee.

After the 235 steps to the bottom of the cavern,
our guide turned off the lights. Total darkness.
"Put your hand in front of your face,
you *think* it's your hand you see."
I had a feeling almost giddy. The mind sees what it wants.
It's why lovers close their eyes when kissing.
I could not see a single thing,
words from my eyes did start. Difficult
for that to continue. Small interruptions—a child's anger,
breakfast dishes, getting toilet paper.

The expected and incalculable distractions—
car pools, dental appointments, the boredom of children.
How easy to give in. To do nothing
and let the hero become the absence
of narration. It's easy the second week
of summer, heat washing the wide streets,

air yellowing over the valley, altocumulus
scattered and sullen, and, of all things, rain
like a crystalline dust spattering the concrete,
leaving a smoky, acrid scent of evaporation.

The child won't get dressed because the clothing
isn't satisfactory. He wants to wear the stretchy
black bike shorts with pink fluorescent stripes
and black tank top he's worn the last three days
on the camping trip. But they're in the wash.
So, naked, he wanders around the house
wailfully because what I have laid out for him—
the seersucker shorts and light blue T-shirt
I thought he'd be cool in—isn't *cool*. What in nature
can be more hurt than him? Just give in.

What if the least daylight could harm him?
His blood photosensitive, so that to live
he had to be kept where it's dark
like the two girls whose strange affliction
was a story I remember from the news
on television. Who only at night could leave
their house banked with lead curtains,
rising to eat breakfast in the dusk,
then going out to play, the moon their sun,
their birds the owls that by day
sleep hidden in the sultry trees.

Give in. For a brief second in the cave,
I thought I glimpsed how we make the world up
with words. How we lie to perfect memory.
After it rained, gnats swarmed through the ruins of light,
the evening turned lustrous. Vireos flitting about

the chamise and bear brush, a few stars in the east.
A small wind stirring the oatgrass, rustling
the digger pines up the slope and the sycamores below
along the creek where two boys, balancing from rock to rock,
crossing the shadows, were ignored in the twilight's slow perishing.

The Last Place

They wake at Rikers at dawn. A guard gives the call. In the nine housing blocks, lights automatically flip on in the dark at 4:30, when the portable meal carts are wheeled to the dorms. Inmates are allowed some minutes for a cat bath before another officer announces breakfast with the cry of "on the chow." Styrofoam trays are passed out then. Each has a plastic spoon with which to stir the thin coffee, to eat the grits, to spread grape jelly on some white bread. Inmates headed for Manhattan Criminal Court finish washing and eating in time to meet a five o'clock bus. Inmates on work details get a few minutes more. By daylight, those on graveyard detail are already suited up in olive green coveralls and sturdy boots and heavy gloves, headed off-island to bury New York's dead.

The administrative code of New York provides that the "Potter's Field shall be under the control of the Department of Corrections," for the burial of deceased paupers. Inmates from Rikers Island provide the labor. Only inmates with less than ninety days of their sentences left to serve are employed. The job is, oddly, considered a plum. For one thing, it involves a change from jailhouse routine. And it's spent out of doors. The pay is the same as for any other inmate detail: 37 cents an hour.

Potter's Field lies on Hart Island. It is not much nautical distance from Rikers, although, in other ways, it can seem like the end of the world. A green Department of Corrections bus carries the graveyard detail. The journey can seem endless as the bus travels north through the neighborhoods of Queens and the Bronx, along an unvarying route to Pelham Parkway. The trip takes more than an hour and, on the ride, an inmate might see more of his city than many New Yorkers ever will. But most spend their bus time asleep. At a goblet-shaped channel the bus crosses a bridge to City Island. I have a friend named Angel who has made this journey a number of times. When I once mentioned to Angel that City Island had been a famous yachting center, with boatyards and careenages and sailmakers' lofts, he looked surprised. "You mean like Gilligan's Island?" he asked.

The bus turns left on narrow Fordham Street and parks at its end by a small trailer adjacent to an iron ferry dock. The dock and the trailer are property of the Department of Corrections. From here the inmates are transported, still aboard the bus, to another small rock in Long Island Sound: Hart Island. Since 1869, the city of New York has used this rock as a burial ground for its indigent dead.

The origin of the term Potter's Field is not absolutely known. One version locates it in scripture: "Then Judas, which had betrayed Him, saw that he was condemned, repented himself and brought again the thirty pieces of silver to the chief priests . . . and they took counsel and bought with them the potters field to bury strangers in." What thirty pieces bought, in local terms, was a small and wooded, melancholy spit of sand and schist covering 101 acres. You can walk its length in just over twenty-five minutes.

Hart Island was originally purchased by the city for $75,000 from the Hunter family, prominent Bronx landholders who had used it as a picnic ground. As many as 800,000 people—those who were paupered or who were cast out or who had no one—now lie buried there. "Blessed are the poor in spirit for theirs is the kingdom of heaven," reads one of the few monuments. "Cry not for us, for we are with the Father. No longer do we cast shadows on the ground as you do."

Inmates on burial duty rarely know more than the name of the bodies they inter. Often, even that is lacking. Work orders accompanying corpses may carry no more identification than "Black female, found east of Bronx River Parkway, 25 years

old" or "Hispanic Male, 42 y.o. (approx), place of death: 241st Street, Inwood." One curious fact that emerges in paperwork accompanying bodies to Hart Island is that people die in public all the time. They die unidentified and nameless. They die lost. They die impoverished, of course, without means for a private burial. Often enough, they die forgotten.

Israel Fallows* is remembered by one man, my friend Angel, a former Rikers inmate who was on the work detail that buried him in the fall of 1989. Israel ended his thirty-six months on earth as a small trussed bundle dropped into the East River. According to the police reports, he was already lifeless when he was weighted with iron rods and placed in the water by his mother's boyfriend. Eventually this man was found guilty of Israel's beating death. But, when first arrested, he was charged with the health code violation "improper disposal of a human body." It was thought then that Israel had died naturally, and that his guardians had been too broke to pay for a funeral. "That wasn't even a violation of the penal code," an assistant to the Bronx District Attorney told me. "The worst we expected him to get at the time was a fine."

In the ten pages of article 205, "Deaths and Disposals of Human Remains," the New York City Health Code details, with morbid decorum, protocols for disposing of dead bodies or their parts. There's delicacy in the code and the language it uses to limit disposition of whole corpses, severed limbs, excised organs. Not every killer bothers with the niceties, of course.

Israel's river burial was inept and sad, but not uncommon. A score of "floaters" turns up in New York harbor every year, most of them dead by the time they hit the water. Presumably, the killers expect the bodies to drift to sea and not, as often happens, catch on rocks or follow the tide to pilings near South Ferry, in the jurisdiction of the First, or "floaters," Precinct. "The truth is there aren't too many ways to dispose of a body in a place as small as New York," a homicide detective explained. "You get a few variations and occasionally something farfetched."

There was nothing farfetched about Israel's end. In its reduced form his story was this: he was abused. Both Israel's mother

---

* Not his real name.

and stepfather had a history of mental problems, and of child abuse and drug abuse, although none of these facts, taken by itself, explains how they came to participate in Israel's death, or why, when his body was released, no one came to claim him. Having photographed and fingerprinted Israel, the coroner placed identification tags on his right big toe and on the zipper of a plastic shroud, called a Shroud-Pak, and eventually placed him in a shallow square box of unfinished pine to join a truckload destined for Hart Island. In 1990, the last year for which figures are available, 1,361 adults were buried at Potter's Field. In that same year, 1,428 infants were laid down there, along with 90 disembodied limbs. As are most unclaimed corpses, Israel's was held by the Medical Examiner's office for somewhat over a week. Adults and children are trucked to Hart Island on alternate days. Israel was buried on a Wednesday, Angel recalls.

Shaped like a heelless boot, Hart Island is just over a mile long, a third of a mile in width. It is flat and marshy on the leeward side and rises on its opposite shore to a low sand bluff. There is a long grayish beach littered with parts of boat hulls and with styrofoam mooring floats and with driftwood. Besides an allée of old locust leading to the modest Corrections Department compound, the trees on the island are mostly scrub. Dense thickets grow over disused burial grids. Wild rose grows in whippy tangles. As plots fill up, new trenches are prepared. Adult bodies are buried now on the southeast side of the island. Children are buried in a separate place 200 yards north. By the year 2000, the entire island will be filled.

In each trench, a long scar the shape and outline of an old-fashioned doorstop, lie forty-eight boxes. Each box is numbered. Even and odd numbers are stacked separately, stepped, three high. The boxes are graduated so that if a body must be exhumed its number can be found and the corpse removed. There are a handful of requests for exhumations each year, by people seeking lost relatives. Only rarely are they found. "It's happened, I don't know, three times, maybe, in ten years," a corrections officer once told me.

Dirt roads run across Hart Island. Some were once covered with crushed mussels and, in places, the iridescent shells crunch underfoot. The island has had many uses over time. During the

Civil War the federal government used it as a tent camp for Confederate prisoners. Later on, buildings were erected. During the yellow fever epidemic the island became a quarantine. Later still, it housed a charity hospital for indigent women, and then an asylum for the insane, and then a poorhouse, and then a tuberculosis sanitarium for women. In 1904, a reformatory was constructed for male misdemeanants aged sixteen to thirty. This building was used as a jailhouse for prisoners working the Potter's Field detail.

At its height, during the early years of this century, the population of Hart Island topped 2,500. In those days there were greenhouses and baseball diamonds. When Ebbets Field, the Dodgers' stadium in Brooklyn, was demolished, bleachers were brought to Hart Island; two rows still stand bolted to a concrete platform in a scruffy sandlot. Weeds poke up through the slats.

The stone structures are abandoned. During a fiscal crisis in the 1970s, the island went entirely untended for a time, and vandals who came by boat uprooted stones and set fires. They raided ledgers that had moldered for decades in disused buildings. Many records and many names from the earliest years of Potter's Field are lost. The Civil War dead are recorded, but only because they had been disinterred and moved to a gravesite in Queens. A white-painted obelisk dated May 30, 1877, and installed by Reno Post 44 of the Army Reserve memorializes these veteran Union soldiers and sailors tersely: "Honor the Brave."

Before I made a visit to Hart Island late last fall, I talked to Angel about Israel Fallows. "I had seen his name in the papers," Angel said. We were sitting in the kitchen of his apartment in the Mott Haven section of the Bronx. "I was in jail at that time," he went on. "They had me in for four months and I had done all the time but thirty days. I didn't really follow the story. But I remembered the name. Why? I don't know. But I remember thinking how his parents must have given him such abuse. It wounded me. Why would they do that? Why would they bug out? I thought about that, but I didn't have an answer. What I mostly thought to myself was 'Wow, this kid never had much of a chance.'"

The Hart Island ferry pulled up to the Fordham Street dock. A deckhand looped a line around a fat green bollard and fastened it

with a clove hitch. While waiting for the Rikers bus, which was late, I sat with several corrections officers inside the small trailer that serves as their field headquarters. The trailer had two rooms, two desks, a cabinet, and a houseplant. On the wall hung a navigation chart showing good fishing spots off a continental shelf called the Hudson Canyon.

"It's 950 fathoms," an officer said.

"That's pretty deep."

"Well, it's over your head."

As is true throughout the jail system, officers carry no weapons on Hart Island. "None of any kind," a sergeant said. "You get a guy grabs your weapon and you're in big trouble. Our major weapon is our mind."

The duty officer held five bullets in his palm and aligned them idly. There will be fourteen inmates today, he said, and four officers, a middling turnout. "The most we ever had was seventeen," he mentioned, as the barred green bus rolled up, just before eight.

The driver was waved aboard the ferry. I followed on foot behind the day's officers. The cold ride across the channel took fifteen minutes, in weather that seemed desolate and biting. The wind drove the waves into low stiff peaks. On the Hart Island side we disembarked, climbed a ladder, and got into a waiting car; the inmates boarded a truck. Then both vehicles headed for the burial trench, where the coffins, which had been shipped over on an earlier ferry, were waiting.

This would be an easy day, said an officer, only eighteen adults going into the ground. "Usually there's at least twenty in a shipment," he said. "Sometimes fifty children arrive at once." One inmate, a redhead, the only white man, was given the job of scribbling a number on each coffin with a red wax crayon. He marked it four times: on the lid, at either end, and on the outward-facing long side. Then a man with a hand-held router gouged the number into the boxtop. The portable generator used to power the router filled the air with an angry, nasal whine.

The inmates stacked the bodies quickly: unknown male black, 21 West 137th Street, received from Manhattan Hearse; Theodore Mason, male white, age unknown; Lenwood Sanders, fifty-six years old, 308 West 114th Street; Alfred Smidiewski; James Thomas;

Virginia Evans; unknown Hispanic male; unknown male black. Two dummy boxes were included to even the piles.

As the inmates built little ziggurats, three to the left and three to the right, an officer shouted, "Let's get some dirt and start filling." I'd been told that the standard knotty pine boxes were just thirteen inches deep. I was struck now by how little room a body takes up. To my eyes, the burial trench seemed shallow, as if the toothed backhoe had merely scarred the earth.

An inmate wearing a bandanna turned to me then and said, "It's not bad work, if you get used to the smell of it. You have to put them someplace, right? You get the fresh air, and I like it better than staying in jail. If you do a good morning, you can have the afternoon to yourself. The only thing I can't take is the babies. I never like that. The babies drive me crazy. Every time I throw a shovel of dirt on one of those boxes, I think to myself: How in the world could they end up in a place like this?"

Cul de Sac

It seems scarcely accidental
that the more peculiar places fill in
as the most natural ones.
This morning they removed the street
beside the house, but left behind
its barely perceptible grade
and curve. Now the
bus stops have moved again

and forcibly transposed every coming and going
into an event I recognize.
The avenue *is* completely different.
And with it, this vista of you I never knew it held,
framed by maples cleared away
just as their turning became visible.
Even while you're here, you're here
and gone, taking care to locate the ways
that reveal a cityscape you can bear.
You've designed it—I mean
doesn't one design
a place by walking around in it?
By accidental discovery,

through cults of wandering,
along self-imposed detours,
I've located passages visceral to me
as the right-handedness of our embrace,
to later find they harbor disorientation
beyond recovery: intersecting parallels,
boundaries I can't find the edge of.
It seems we're wishing most of the time
for simultaneous existences, but how to respond
when identical discoveries turn up fully intact?
Passages we had located far apart
have revealed themselves linked
at their boundaries.

I'm retracing now
this morning's path, following to a T,
as though something were lost and traceable
en route—an affirmation in a way.
But the business of the day is removal,
and the city's issuing permits by the dozen.
Now, even as I approach you,
the blocks are breaking loose
from their perpendiculars;
even as I arrive, the neighborhood ends
in its own center.

Language Lessons

This evening when he comes into the house, the spoon is stuck. It's wedged so tightly into the wood that I abandon it. I stumble up the stairs, groping at the risers, and find him already seated at the table, drying his hands on his rough shirt.

"Where were you, boy!?" he shouts, and grabs me by my wrist.

I struggle not to pull against him. "I was looking for onions in the cellar."

"Liar!" he says playfully, and cuffs me. "Did you learn your lessons?"

I nod. "Yes sir."

"That's what matters," he says. "Now get me my food."

I dish him out a mutton chop that has been cooking all afternoon. Sitting across the table from him, I watch his large jaws work up and down against the stringy meat.

His mouth is enormous. At the end of the meal he yawns, and I watch as his lips pull back, his jaws part, and the space blooms into a huge emptiness. I hold tightly to my chair, leaning forward, and look. At the base of his mouth, where his throat begins, are clouds the color of the dirty sheep he once bought after the rains flooded our fields. It was such a bountiful harvest that we were able to buy new clothes and an old truck. The clouds scurry across the gap between the mountains of my father's teeth. Beneath the cloud cover there are rich fields divided into even plots of squares, rectangles, and circles.

In the fields I can barely discern farmers about their business. Along a road I notice a man shouldering a heavy burden while his wife walks hurriedly at his side. She carries a child on her back. I imagine the child looks up with sleepy, fretful eyes and sees the clouds part and my eyes peering down at him like moons.

My father shuts his mouth and peels his skin slowly from his worn body. He walks to the corner and hangs the suit of skin carefully on its brass hook and comes back to the table. The skin leaves a smell in the air like the inside of a boot. Underneath his skin is a harder shell of shining bone as smooth as a tortoise's back. He plucks his eyes out and holds them in one hand.

"Bring me a glass of water," he says.

I fetch a cup for him. He fumbles for the table with his free hand. I guide that hand to the cup. He picks up the eyes and drops them in the silty water, which splashes onto his hand.

He reaches out for me, but I stand beyond his grasp. "Where's my pipe, boy!?" he says.

I look at the holes where his eyes belong. "Upstairs, in your room."

Using his hands, he guides himself toward the stairs that lead to our rooms. "Hurry up, boy. Wash up, and then we can deal with your studies." He crawls up the stairs.

I glance down at the eyes. They are moving about the cup, looking at the sharp white edges and the tiny pieces of brown silt that cloud the fluid. I lean over them, fascinated. They roll around in the water and catch me staring. I move a little to one side and together they turn with me, the way the fish in our pond move all as one body even if you startle them with your shadow. I step back a bit. The eyes push up to the edge of the water, straining to lift themselves over the lip of the cup, all the time watching me. In a fright, I take down a book of words from the shelf and settle at the opposite end of the table. Slowly, from the very start, I begin to recite the meanings of things.

•   •   •

After my father returns with his pipe, we sit at the table by the light of a single candle. He keeps the cup in front of him, and the eyes bob at the surface. The water seems to whiten from the eyes, as if drops of milk had been stirred into the cup. The eyes ripple the surface of the water like minnows, straining to have a better look. He asks me about the words I have learned today. I tell him in English, but he scowls.

He leans toward me, lighting his pipe. The smoke clouds one empty socket and he covers the space with a dangling lid. Both eyes splash about in the cup to have a look at me.

"Universe?" he says, and relights the stubborn pipe.

"Mirozdaniye," I mumble. World house.

"Spark?"

"Iskra."

"Fire?"

"Which one?" I say slyly.

"Just fire," he grumbles.

"Ogon."

"God?"

I don't look at him. "Chort!"

He reaches across the table and stuffs one eye back in his head. I cringe when he turns it on me. He reaches out and slaps my face so hard it knocks me to the floor. "That's the devil, stupid!"

I stare up at him and feel tears bubble in the corners of my eyes. Holding them back as best I can, I get up. I sit back down and tap my fingertips lightly on the tabletop. The single eye in the cup turns toward me and I feel like reaching in and crushing it in my fist.

My father stares at me and rises. "Mind your lessons and your mouth! Otherwise you'll be as stupid as a rock for the rest of your life." He turns quickly and disappears upstairs to his bed.

The remaining eye splashes about in the cup as its master vanishes. It turns toward me and freezes. I lean menacingly above it and blow out the candle. The flame leaves a spot where it was, still glowing in the darkness. Into the quiet I whisper, "Muha, muha, na stenye, kock vyj pozhavayjete?" ("Fly, fly, on the wall, how's life?")

• • •

The second day, after my father departs, I place the eye he leaves for me on the windowsill overlooking the fields. I begin diligently enough, learning the day's words under its scrupulous gaze. Then I finish my breakfast of a hard roll and sweetened coffee, and descend into the cellar. The light filters through the mudsills and casts an orange light like melted wax on the dirt walls of the cellar. I wedge myself against the center beam where the spoon is buried in the damp wood, and pry against the spoon.

It won't budge.

I put all my weight against it but only bend the handle. Finally, I go off to hunt for a tool with which to pry it out. On the shelves there are empty paint cans, boxes of family photographs, spools of green wire, a welding torch, stacks of rotting lumber, dead mice, bottles of ancient beer that my father once made, a broken plow harrow, a box of chipped coffee cups, and sticky, dusty spiderwebs stitching the whole mess together. I take down the toolbox for the welding kit. On the shelf behind the box is a nest of white ivy that has snaked its way in through the foundation and now grows without the help of the sun.

The ivy must be cracking the foundation, I realize. I straighten one vine so it will grow straight up into our floor.

In the toolbox is a pair of rusted vise grips with flat jaws, for holding hot metal. I adjust the tool to the thin blade of the spoon and clamp the jaws shut. First I straighten the handle of the spoon, then I pull. The spoon gives way instantly.

I return the tools to their place and go back to my own work. The morning light warms the room like fire licking at a bubbling soup pot. I think of the soups I know: potato, leek, wild mushroom, borscht. I imagine the hole in the wood to be the soup pot. I pretend to pour in water, potatoes, celery, garlic, turnips, carrots, bay leaves, salt, and ground peppercorns, then let the broth simmer. I widen the pot with my spoon, chipping away the wood, then strain the broth and throw away the cooked vegetables. I toss in dried wild mushrooms, beets, lemon juice, and a dash of sugar, and let the sunlight do its work.

When the soup seems almost perfect, I take off my ears and fingers and throw them in. I pluck off my nose and my thumbs and add them too. Soon off come the hands, the hair, the feet, the teeth, arms, legs, and eyes. As the pot bubbles furiously under the turn of the spoon, I hurl myself over the edge and sink into the bubbling borscht.

When I serve him at the end of the day, he compliments me by saying that the soup is the best I have ever made.

• • •

That night we go over the words quickly.
"Silence?" he asks.
"Molchaniye."
"Water?"
"Voda."
"Hope?"
"Nadezhda."

He rubs his hands together and they grind lightly so that sparks fly off his calloused palms. He asks me to fetch a book from the shelf next to the fireplace. I take the candle from the table and find the one he wants. It is the story, he explains, of an orphan being raised by his aunt. My father describes in detail how the boy desires to follow his schoolteacher to a nearby city and become learned. My father holds up the boy far over my head as an example. I look up into the shadows of the ceiling between the heavy beams. The orphan's ghost dives in and out of the tatters of cobwebs above me. He reaches down a tiny, pale hand, but my father interrupts me before I leave.

"Read this," he says, and hands the book to me.

"Where do I start?"

"From the top, here," he says, and points with his thick finger. He sits back and runs his hands roughly against the smooth wood of the table. They make a sound like sandpaper.

I read, but the words are like a dull babble in which the image of our ruined house appears as if it were made out of smoke. I think of the progress of the hole today. Perhaps if I widen the soft, lower corner a bit tomorrow and the next day and the next, I can level the house in another week. The hole is now the size of a fist. I think of the word in Russian for ruin: *razoryeniye*. It rolls on my tongue like a piece of sugar and I swallow it down cheerfully. But then the smoke clears and the image dissolves as a passage of the book startles me to thought. I read it again: "He had meditated much and curiously on the probable sort of process that was involved in turning the expressions of one language into those of another. He concluded that a grammar of the required tongue would contain, primarily, a rule, prescription, or clue of the nature of a secret cipher, which, once known, would enable him, by merely applying it, to change at will all words of his own speech into those of the foreign one. . . ."

I nod at the sense this makes.

I look up at my father. He is smiling at me and his eyes blaze with sarcasm.

He closes the book for me and returns it to the shelf. There will be no more words tonight.

• • •

On the fourth day I find to my delight that the wood is so rotten the beam gives way by mid-morning. I carefully spoon out as much of the wood pulp as I can, then smash the beam with a piece of scrap lumber. However, the house is stubborn. The floor sags with a shriek and I run outside screaming. I stand in the shadows of the yard and throw rocks at the porch, careful not to break the windows. But the house stands exactly as it had before. Finally, I go back in. The only sign of damage I find is a large sinking spot in the middle of the kitchen floor, just over the supporting beam.

I yank out a patch of brown hair. He'll kill me, I think. Scrambling around the kitchen, skirting the sunken floor, my thoughts nag at my feet like hungry mice. I imagine him lifting me over his head and snapping my body in two like a bit of kindling. I hear the eye moving about in its cup on the kitchen windowsill. It turns and watches as I charge into the depression. I smash the sunken floor with a chair, but nothing happens except that the chair explodes into splinters, and I collapse in a heap amidst the broken wood. The eye leaps out of its cup and rolls across the floor toward me, winding its way through the debris. I grind my dirty fists into my own eyes until the tears stop. The clock strikes four in the hallway, the four chimes saying: late, late, late, late.

I stand up and get the matches. The eye rolls alongside me like a worried dog.

The blaze starts easily. The flames lick at the broken chair, then dance merrily along as they find new things to feed upon. The eye hides underneath the baseboards by the door. I feed the fire the curtains from over the sink, a stack of yellowed newspapers, dishtowels, napkins, kitchen knives, plates, an antique lamp, yellowing portraits of my ancestors which hang along the stove wall, my father's slippers, his pipe, cookbooks, all the silverware, including the aluminum digging spoon, and even manage to push the dining room table into the well of fire. The flames take all of this happily. I put my hands into the fire and we dance wickedly about the kitchen, each trying to outdo the other with flips and whirls. But the fire eventually becomes jealous of my ability to jump higher and quicker than it ever can and chases me out of the house. I manage to lock the eye in for a fine view.

I go out on the steps and wait for the fire to eat its fill.

•   •   •

He arrives while the fire is still hot and angry. He takes one frightened glance at the house, then one at me.

"How did this happen?" he screams.

I shake my head in wonder.

He bellows like a wounded animal, digging at the empty socket in his face as a shower of sparks ascends toward the darkening sky. He takes off his belt and drags me to the tree in the center of our yard. He cuts loose the rope that holds my swing, lashes me to the tree with it, then methodically whips me with the belt. I try not to smile as the house collapses in a blaze of cinders. He doesn't stop until the welts bleed.

"What is the word for sorrow?" he screams at me.

"Lyubof!" I scream right back.

"Not love, you idiot, sorrow!"

"Lyubof! Lyubof!" I scream, and each word leaves a long scar on my back.

•   •   •

On the fifth and sixth days he drags me with him to work in the fields, though I stubbornly resist any temptation to assist in his work. I lean over my shovel and glare at him, while the flies cluster over my shirt to have a chance at my wounds. He weeds and waters the long rows of green shoots that have just found their way into the sunlight. When he happens to look up and sees me standing by, he swears and taunts me. "Stop feeling sorry for yourself and get to work." I bend down and pluck a few weeds from the rows of shoots, but soon I straighten and watch the crows dancing in the air over the dark wood that borders the river.

At night we sleep in the barn with the animals. I curl up into the straw like a cat, listening to their soft voices. A barn swallow hops down beside me, sticks its beak in my ear, and begins to tell me a lie. Each word is as small as a grain of sand.

I brush her away, but in a moment she's back.

"In a certain village," she whispers, "not far, not near, not high, and not low, there lived a fool whose father and mother were so tired of his breaking things, laying about on the stove, and getting beaten by the neighbors that they gave him a hundred rubles to go out into the world and leave them in peace. The fool, not knowing any better, took the money and left. He wandered about the countryside until he grew tired of starving or being run off by farmers and went into the city of Kiev. Immediately upon his arrival, he saw a man being hanged . . ."

"Hanged?" I interrupt her with a whisper.

She continues as if I'd never spoken. "The fool, never having seen such a thing before, asked someone what the man was being hanged for. The stranger looked at the fool with curiosity and explained that the hanging was for the man's wickedness, that he was a hero in the tsar's court who had bedded the tsarina while the leader was away in battle. So, asked the fool, he is being hanged for pleasure? The stranger only laughed and walked away."

I twist my head away from this, but she hops after me and the whispering starts again.

"That night, the fool went to a tavern and drank himself into a stupor. One of the women there took him upstairs to her bed. The woman tore the clothes from the fool's back before she took her pleasure with him. She ripped his shirt right down the middle and threw the torn halves on the floor and he was free."

I wonder what she means, but don't ask.

"Then she took her pleasure with his rough body and simple ways. When the fool woke in the morning, he remembered the scene of the hanging, and ran outside and found himself a piece of rope in the yard. He walked away into the woods and was never seen again."

"Why such sadness?" I ask her in a whisper.

"What's that?" my father asks and turns his single eye on me.

The swallow hops away, brushing its wings on my face, and flies off into the gloom of the barn.

"Nothing," I say.

He grumbles something in Russian. "Then sleep."

I carefully tuck the swallow's story, still warm from the telling, in the folds of my coat and sleep.

• • •

On the seventh day he tells me he has had enough of my laziness. He takes a single shovel and a burlap sack from the barn. He drags me out to the fields and forces me to dig a deep hole. While I dig, he stands over me.

"Do you remember the things I taught you?"

I throw a shovelful on his boot.

He reaches down and grabs me by the hair.

"Struggle?" he snaps at me.

"Borba," I say, and try to throw another shovelful at him.

He simply steps back. "Emptiness?"

"Nool."

"Darkness?"

"Smyert."

"You're an idiot," he groans, and pushes me back to my work. I dig until the walls of the hole rise above my head. "That's enough," he says.

I scramble back out and he grabs me. He wrestles me into the burlap sack, cursing me as he does it. Once he manages this trick, he ties the top tight with a piece of rope and tosses me into the hole. I land hard and it stuns me.

When I come to, I feel something soft and familiar bump me. It takes me a moment to realize that it's soil. He's burying me! I scream at the top of my lungs, begging him to give me another chance.

"I'd sooner burn in hell!" he shouts at me.

"One more chance, for God's sake! Father!? Father!?"

But in a moment he's got the job done. The light goes out and there is only the smell of the earth and burlap, and the soft sound of my own breath coming back to me like a familiar whisper. I hear his boots crunch against soil overhead. He is walking away!

I try to remember the prayers I taught myself from one of my father's books, but the words scatter like crows startled out of the fields.

At first it is not difficult to breathe, but soon enough each breath feels as if tiny nails are being driven carefully into my chest. I can hear the sound of earthworms gathering around the hole, their tiny mouths probing the soil for the smell of my skin. There are only a few minutes to find a way out.

I think of the word for hole. "Dira!" I whisper and the word goes spinning vainly along the inside edge of the canvas, guiding my hand for a rent in the rough fabric.

It's hopeless, I think. I realize I need a stronger word.

The sparrow's story begins to peck violently at my chest. I reach into my coat, carefully unwrapping the story, and one by one the words struggle free of their little net of meaning. They swarm around my head like bees until one alights on the tip of my forefinger. The word begins to tug at my hand, raising it to the canvas. "Tear! Tear! Tear!" it screams in its tiny voice.

I remember in my confusion how the woman had torn the fool's shirt off his back. The word puts my hand against the canvas. Then it spins down and lifts my other hand to sit beside its brother. "Tear!" the word shouts again, and I pull as hard as I can.

In a moment the bag gives way. In another I have the bag torn wide enough for me to escape. I pull down huge handfuls of dirt on myself. The soil rains down like thick hail, each handful choking and blinding me. I don't even stop to breathe. The earth feels like it has turned upside down. I imagine myself standing on my head, digging myself into the belly of the earth, and stop in a panic. I take a quick breath and my head clears. At last my hands pop out into the air like new shoots. I yank myself free of the hole and collapse against the dirt.

Overhead the sun is burning a hole in the center of the sky.

I rest for a few minutes to catch my breath and stop shaking. My clothes are covered with dirt, but I sit still, trembling, and wait for the sun to warm me. It is a long time before I can even stand. I stumble down to the river and wash the soil off my face and hands. Afterward, I sit on the riverbank and look into the distance. Beyond the far side of the river is a road I've never noticed before, disappearing into the edge of the dark wood. I imagine crossing over to the other side of the water, cursing him as I go. Perhaps I could follow the road into the wood, find something to eat, someone who might help me.

But the journey ends there. After a long time I stand up, brush myself off, and walk slowly back to where my father is working. He is not in the least surprised to see me and even raises his hand in greeting. He shows me what has to be done. It is a long and terrible day of work.

The Dream of Phernazes

In the midst of war—imagine, Greek poems.
C. P. Cavafy

Within the harsh reflections on the stone was heard
my own hollow hand; I wrote all day
and it was tired

the violence of composition torments me, at times I wonder
if it is worth the laurels, honors,
and money I make

the commissioned poem had been finished
for the cunning and kill-loving ancestor
of our honored king—
when they brought me the distressing news
of the Roman advance (I am very much afraid
I must soon learn good Latin)

Suddenly I recalled last night's dream
which I had completely forgotten—I don't really believe
in dreams, oracles, and prophecies
(no doubt they hold people in line)

I'll write as many as you wish

I had seen that, burdened with news of the future,
I appeared in the sleep of the amateur
and later famous Alexandrian poet Cavafy

it was a May afternoon of '17, I noticed in the calendar,
he was half-asleep, troubled in his chair—he must have also
been writing some poem of his all day;
I found the opportunity (in a moment sliding
secretly out of his dream) and slipped into the city

Only the Egyptian sun appeared to sink in the harbor
absolutely undisturbed—everywhere around me
from all points of the compass the stench of carnage,
quarrels divided my brothers in language
and in the homeland an untimely reflection
of endless refugees already darkened
the eyes; the uproar in the market was indescribable,
a great evil, something like the change foretold in distant Scythia

I was coming back lost in thought, my throat dry;
undoubtedly such conditions would cause
constant delays in the poet's plans

I would have liked to ask him many things before I returned, when

suddenly I saw at the road's edge
rushing at me from the trenches of sleep
that same Cavafy
his gentle face unknowable
a gas mask

To my dear slave who was terrified by the shouts and came running
I quickly put the question that occupied me

What could the poet have been thinking all day
as he wrote his poem?

I certainly expect no answer from anyone
—who can understand this profession
in days like ours?

The Family of Greeks

Who does not remember that poem
for Greeks who forgot
love, St. George Oedipus
nailing his dragon father in the mouth
to wed his mother's tongue
freely?
does the king live? now in seas the idiot mermaid
looks for him, his sister, his daughter

Who does not remember that poem
for Greeks who forgot themselves in the past
or went away in the diaspora of another tongue
the great homeland grew smaller, smaller,
they stuffed their narrow throats with ancient phrases
"EVERYTHING IN MEDIOCRITY," now you hear
unloved Sphynx and illiterate Virgin
how to make children
who don't talk back

Who does not remember that poem
beginning so precisely

Measure of all, man is nothing
He forgets everything
Let him remember that

Translated by David Mason and the author

Iphigenia at Aulis

Directed by Ariane Mnouchkine

◆

The Bacchae

Directed by Ingmar Bergman

Iphigenia at Aulis

Director
Ariane Mnouchkine

Music
Jean-Jacques Lemêtre

Translation
Jean and Mayotte Bollack

Scene Design
Guy-Claude François

Costume Design
Nathalie Thomas

Cast of Characters

Agamemnon: Simon Abkarian
Menelaus: Bernard Martin
Achilles: Simon Abkarian
First Messenger: Brontis Jodorowsky
Second Messenger: Georges Bigot

Iphigenia: Nirupama Nityanandan
Clytemnestra: Juliana Carneiro da Cunha
Old Man: Georges Bigot
Leader of the Chorus: Catherine Schaub

p. 153 Ariane Mnouchkine rehearsing members of the chorus

p. 154 Members of the chorus

p. 155 Members of the chorus

p. 156 The leader of the chorus directing a dance

p. 157 The leader of the chorus

p. 158 Iphigenia dancing around Agamemnon

p. 159 Clytemnestra and Iphigenia

Iphigenia at Aulis opened at the Théâtre du Soleil, Paris, on November 16, 1990.

153

The Bacchae

Director
Ingmar Bergman

Music
Daniel Börtz

Translation
Jan Stolpe and Göran O. Eriksson

Scene and Costume Design
Lennart Mörk

Choreography
Donya Feuer

Dramaturge
Ulla Åberg

Cast of Characters

Dionysus: Sylvia Lindenstrand   *Agave:* Anita Soldh
Tiresias: Laila Andersson-Palme   *First Messenger:* Per Mattson
Cadmus: Sten Wahlund   *Second Messenger:* Peter Stormare
Pentheus: Peter Mattei   *Leader of the Bacchantes:* Berit Lindholm

p. 161   Ingmar Bergman leading a rehearsal

p. 162   The leader of the Bacchantes

p. 163   The Bacchantes dancing during the earthquake

p. 164   Dionysus

p. 165   A Bacchante destroying the effigy of Pentheus

p. 166   The Second Messenger recounting the death of Pentheus

p. 167   Cadmus and Agave with the head of Pentheus

p. 168   Dionysus with sacrificial goat

The Bacchae opened at the Royal Swedish Theater of Stockholm on November 2, 1991.

Iphigenia at Aulis & The Bacchae

Euripides is a strange combination of lateness, perhaps even decadence, in style and primitivism in content. He is more elusive in his values than the granitic Aeschylus, less sharp in his oppositions than Sophocles. Nietzsche characterized Euripides as the man who seized on the myth of Dionysus and Apollo—the foundation of the tragic form—rescuing it one last time from "the stern, intelligent eyes of an orthodox dogmatism" in order to make use of it again for tragedy. "What did you want, sacrilegious Euripides, when you sought to compel this dying myth to serve you once more? It died under your violent hands—and then you needed a copied masked myth that . . . merely knew how to deck itself out in the ancient pomp." In Euripides the old tragedy barely survives except as "a monument of its exceedingly painful and violent death."

Strangely enough, Euripides' very last tragedies, *The Bacchae* and *Iphigenia at Aulis,* are works that self-consciously return in subject matter to some scarcely remembered beginning point, an early and yet profoundly disturbing clue to what Yeats called "the uncontrollable mystery on the bestial floor." *The Bacchae* presents the advent of Dionysus, an Asiatic outsider to Mount Olympus, a god of uncertain but nevertheless menacing sexuality, who wreaks havoc upon Pentheus, the skeptical young king of Thebes who has succeeded Cadmus and now refuses to admit Dionysus as a god. The climax comes with an extraordinary speech, in which the Second Messenger recounts how Agave, Pentheus's mother and a pliant convert to the Dionysiac cult, has killed her own son in an ecstatic fit, tearing him limb from limb. Convinced that she has savagely mutilated a lion, Agave then leads a procession of Bacchantes onto the stage, bearing her son's head in her hand like a proud trophy. Not only is Pentheus's palace also burned in the process, but Thebes itself is changed utterly. Dionysus is triumphant, but at scarcely imaginable cost.

In *Iphigenia* Euripides situates his drama at the point immediately prior to the Trojan War. The Greek armies, led by the sons of Atreus, Agamemnon and Menelaus—one the husband of

Clytemnestra, father to Iphigenia, Electra, and Orestes, the other the husband of Helen—are about to embark for Asia, but are delayed by a dead calm at the port of Aulis. Calchas the prophet has informed Agamemnon that only if his daughter is sacrificed to the goddess of Aulis will the forces be able to sail. Stubbornly committed to his military campaign, Agamemnon proceeds to lure his wife and children from Mycenae to Aulis, pretending that the young Iphigenia is being summoned to a wedding with Achilles. Clytemnestra discovers that her daughter is to be murdered and naturally resists; as Euripides unfolds the drama of mother, daughter, and father, the seeds are visibly planted of the resentment and revenge that will later propel Clytemnestra not only to adultery but to the murder of Agamemnon, exactly those bloodily tragic actions that had furnished the action of Aeschylus's *Oresteia*. *Iphigenia* ends with the young girl's willing, not to say saintlike, self-sacrifice to her father's ambitions, even as she walks away from her grieving mother. "Dance," she says to the chorus:

> Let us dance in honor of Artemis,
> Goddess, queen and blest.
> With my own blood
> In sacrifice
> I will wash out
> The fated curse of God.
> O Mother, my lady mother,
> Now I give you my tears
> For when I come to the holy place
> I must not weep.

Despite their awful, terror-filled action, these plays make the heart visible, as Marianne McDonald phrases it in her book on modern cinematic versions of Euripides. True, the lineaments of age-old myth are as easily discernible here as they are in Sophocles and Aeschylus, but Euripides is much more the ethnographer of the situation, more the exposer of guile and manipulation, more the psychologist of victimization and self-delusion than either of his two great predecessors. Thus one does not feel at the end of *The Bacchae* and *Iphigenia* the same sense of reconciliation and closure often found in earlier tragedies. Partly because of his relative lateness, Euripides uses his plays to repeat, reinterpret, return to, and revise his somewhat familiar material; but the peculiar sensation of the Euripidean tragedy is its playfulness, if by *play* one has in mind the prolongation of effort, the disinterested and almost purely formal gestures he uses to elaborate, extend, embellish, and illustrate the tragic action. One senses in Euripides both a vital modern psychology and a quasi-abstract delight taken in configurations of characters, situations, rhetoric.

This does not make his work less urgent and disturbing as a result, but more. When, after having devastated Thebes and the house of Cadmus, Dionysus discloses himself, there is, I believe, a uniquely appalling force in his words of self-revelation, as if he is perfectly prepared to go on playing with, harassing, and finally destroying the mortals who have slighted (but not seriously wronged) him. Euripides is as much the poet of that sadism as he is the melodist of Iphigenia's victimhood, her advocate against Agamemnon's ghastly tricks and macho insistence. When Nietzsche said of Euripides that he rescued the old and dying myths only to destroy them, he meant not only that Euripides dares to humanize what was distant and nonhuman, but that Euripides imparts a human logic—a structure of vitality—to gods and heroes who would otherwise have remained outside time and beyond place.

Theatricality and music are the elements in Euripidean tragedy most compelling to contemporary directors. Andrzey Wajda's 1989 version of Sophocles' *Antigone* was designed as a political commentary on the transformation of Poland by Solidarity. Despite their great power, such interpretive parallelisms are inimical to Euripides, whose late works stage passion and cunning as musical variations on each other. In her tremendously daring production of *The Atrides,* the French director Ariane Mnouchkine uses *Iphigenia* as a prologue to Aeschylus's *Oresteia.* She converts the Théâtre du Soleil, a long and narrow, shedlike structure in Vincennes, outside Paris, into a rectangular bullring and compels it to serve as a sort of Bayreuth where ritual, music, and astonishingly compelling stylized acting combine to represent the fall of a house doomed by genealogy and temperament to horrific deeds.

The heart of Mnouchkine's conception is the chorus, eighteen to twenty dancers costumed alike, whether men or women, in robes, knee-pads, and fantastic black, red, and white makeup. The settings and their provenance suggest a sort of anthropological, quasi-folkloric Near East; they dance in rows that seem to have broken off from the circular order of a Near Eastern *dabke,* although Mnouchkine's dancers are much more athletic and brash than *dabke* dancers. Her principal actors and actresses are ecstatic declaimers, yet for all their tremendous composition of gesture and language, they are outshone by the extraordinary Catherine Schaub, who leads the chorus. Catlike, elusive, smiling, and secret, she summons, leads, badgers, and dares the chorus, as well as the actors, with demonic recitations, yelps, anguished cries. Only she, among the choric ensemble, speaks. At the conclusion of the play, all—even the sacrificed Iphigenia and her mother—return to the stage and dance in an ecstatic, twenty-minute-long curtain call to the insistent rhythms of a percussion band (gongs, drums, cymbals, triangles, xylophones) punctuated by an occasional horn and, at the final moment, the barking of dogs.

Where Mnouchkine's *Iphigenia* is conceived as a ballet with strophic interventions, Ingmar Bergman's production of *The Bacchae* is staged as an opera at Stockholm's Royal Opera House. The music is by Daniel Börtz, a Swedish serialist composer. Dionysus is played by a woman, whose beauty and gymnastic strength further underscore the god's polymorphousness and dynamic scope. Like Mnouchkine's, Bergman's involvement in the production is total. Each of the choric Bacchantes, for example, is given a name, life history, and character, lifting them from collective anonymity to personalized involvement. The lyric ensemble is broken only intermittently, as when Peter Stormare as the Second Messenger narrates the dismemberment of Pentheus in spoken, as opposed to sung, verse. Less a ritualized than a familiarized version of Euripides' great masterpiece, Bergman's *Bacchae* heightens the terror of destruction and sorrow by giving the sense that each of the personages on stage has had the Dionysiac experience separately. As in his films, the impersonal and the heroic are transfigured downward, so to speak, into everyday lives and informal happenings.

These two contemporary revivals of Euripides do not in fact bring him closer to us, even though they are performed in modern languages (French and Swedish). In both instances one feels that the director intends an alienating effect, as if to say that we should not come too near to or identify too easily with characters so manifestly ravaged by the rarest of dark forces and dark hearts. And this also has the effect of emphasizing what was already strange and out of season about Euripides in 410 B.C., when these plays were first performed. He dramatizes the intersection of myth and reality, where each turns upon and challenges the other. The result is an extraordinary artificiality, performance declaring itself such and drawing attention to itself before an audience perturbed and awed.

—Edward W. Said

From the *Gododdin*

Steady as a grown man
and yet a youth
ablaze for the fighting
fast stallions the manes flying
his legs gripping them
the light shield riding
the lean horse's flank
blue glint of blades
garments with gold borders
there will never be
bitterness between us
but I will make a song
of you for your fame
the field ran with his blood
before ever he was married
the crows ate their fill
before he was buried
Owain dear friend
covered with crows
the place haunts me with horror
Marro's one son was killed there

Diadem on his forehead
he rode always in front
he was tongue-tied before a girl
he paid for his feasting
his shield is broken
he bore down with the battle cry

on those who ran from him
he fought on while blood flowed
those who faced him he cut like rushes
in great halls the Gododdin will tell
of the return to Madawg's tent
where a hundred rode out only one came home

Diadem on his forehead
a wild wolf's rage
a string of amber at his throat
around and around
he was worth fine amber
in return for the wine he turned their blades back
with the blood running on them
men came from Gwynedd and Gogledd
at the bidding of Ysgyrran's son
and shields were broken to pieces

High were their hearts who went as one to Catraeth
they had drunk fresh mead and it was poison to them
there were three hundred of them drawn up for battle
and after the shouting there was silence
though they went to be forgiven in churches
the truth was that the hand of death was on them

Those who went to Catraeth in the first light
by their own high hearts they were cut off early
they drank the sweet gold mead that ensnared them
for one complete year there had been singing
red their swords leave the blades unwashed
their white shields four-sided spears
before Mynydawg Mwynfawr's men

Those who went to Catraeth were already famous
for all of one year they drank out of gold
wine and mead in honor of their calling
three hundred sixty-three of them in collars of twisted gold
of all those who charged after the mead was gone
three alone fought their way out of the battle
Aeron's two dogs of war and the rock Cynon
and I bleeding my way back to make my song

They went to Catraeth when the drinking was done
I would be ashamed not to sing their story
they fought with red spears they were hounds of war
they stood their ground wielding the dark heavy shafts
living would hardly be bearable to me
if I had left one of Brennych's band with life in him
I lost a friend there but I stood by him
he fought to the end and I grieve at leaving him
there was no dowry that he would come back for
he came from Maen Gwyngwn
Y Cair's last son

They went to Catraeth raising the battle shout
fast horses dark armor and shields
spears raised above them with the points sharpened
chain mail glinting swords flashing
one led the way pushing into the fight
five fifties went down before the blades that followed him
it was Rhufawn Hir who offered gold on the altar
and rewarded well those who sang for him

They went to Catraeth as the day began
there was one bringing bitterness to the enemy
they would need a bier to bear them away

no swords wilder than those that were with him
and never question of asking for quarter
when Neirthiad was leading the Gododdin
he showed the daring of his heart

There was one who went to Catraeth at first light
and a wall of shields rose around him
they charge they make way they lay hands on spoils
the crash of shields echoes like thunder
a burning man a man of judgment a champion
he plunged his spears and he tore with them
his blades butchered in welling blood
his iron came down on heads in the struggle
confronting Erthgi armies would cower

There was one who rushed to the battle
before the cows were awake
you had the way of a lion
the mead was gone there was only courage
a proud leader who would give no ground
son of Boddw Adaf renowned Eithinyn

They charged as one they rushed to be fighting
they were drunk with pure mead their lives were short
Mynydawg's men who won fame as warriors
for their fill of mead they laid down their lives
Cardawg and Madawg and Pyll and Ieuan
Gwgan and Gwiawn and Gwyn and Cynfan
Peredur with steel in his fist Gwawdur and Aeddan
where the fight swirled they stood firm and smashed shields
and though death bore them down they dealt it again
not one of them returned to what he knew

When you were famous for the way you fought
for our grain fields in the highlands
we were looked up to because we were with you
heavy door fortress for holding out
and a hand always for those who called to him
he was the tower in which the army trusted
wherever he was they called it heaven

As Catlew said no man
had a horse to catch Marchlew
he set spears in the thick of the fight
from a huge horse charging
not one to stand for the packsaddles
he struck out with a savage sword
with a fist like a block he dug in the ash-wood shafts
from the back of his foaming stallion
a beloved prince a free hand pouring the wine for us
swinging the whetted blade on which the blood flew
it was like the scything in haying weather
the way Marchlew let blood

His fame came from the south with him
Isaac whose ways were like a tide coming in
bounteous and open
fine friend to drink with
where his weapon went
a story ended
in his rage there was pure rage alone
his blade echoed in the heads of mothers
there was honor for Gwydneu's son
a wall in the battle

The one thing dearest the saddest loss
all for feasting all for a land
already taken and wasted
all for the hair that falls from a head
in the fight there was an eagle that was Gwydyen
he fought with his spear for Gwyddug
in the hands of a farmer
Morien's spear took out of the way
three wild boars with death before them
and Myrddin of the songs was with us
whose gift held up our hearts
when the walls rang and the fight tightened
with Saxons Irish Picts
and Gwenabwy fab Gwen the quick-handed
carried off Bradwen's rigid red body

I have not the burdens of the high-born
I am not looking for vengeance
my legs stretched out
under the crawlers
in the house of earth
an iron chain
around my ankles
brought on by mead by drinking horn
by the raid on Catraeth
I am not laughing
I Aneirin am not I
let Taliesin tell it
whom the words obey
I sang to the Gododdin
before the day

Translated by W. S. Merwin

Translator's Note

The poem known as the *Gododdin*, as it has reached our time, consists of 103 stanzas. They are remains from a vigorous oral tradition of indeterminate age, and are thought to date from the sixth century. When or in what circumstances they were first written down is unknown. One manuscript from the ninth or tenth century, with forty-two sections, and one from the thirteenth century, with eighty-eight sections, make up what is called *The Book of Aneirin*, the half-legendary poet to whom the sequence of elegies is attributed. Almost nothing is known of him for certain, and part of the legend derives from the poem itself.

In ancient Welsh literature narrative was matter for prose. The battle of Catraeth, or Catterick, was not recounted as an epic. Instead, the story emerges from the individual elegiac lyrics.

The Gododdin is the name of a Celtic people whose descendants would be Welsh. At the time of the events in the poem, they were living in an area of what is now northern Scotland, already outnumbered by the invading English, who had taken the region of Catraeth, to the south of Edinburgh, and built fortifications there. A king of the Gododdin, Mynydawg Mwynfawr, as the story goes, recruited a band of more than three hundred warriors picked from the men of Celtic Britain and assembled them at his court in Edinburgh. There they were royally feasted for a year, and prepared themselves for battle. Finally they rode out to Catraeth, to try to retake it against virtually hopeless odds. The accounts of the end of the battle differ: one, or three, or very few—Aneirin among them—survived. The court, the preparations, and some of the heroes of the fight are among the rudiments of the legend of the Round Table and the Arthurian cycle about a kingdom that will be reborn.

I know no Welsh, though I grew up surrounded by the sound of it and its glorious accent in English. I read several accounts of the Arthurian story as a child, of course, and read Welsh poetry in translation from the time I discovered it in college. I had known the bewitching Welsh tales of the *Mabinogion* for almost as long. Familiarity with their light and world had been more or less taken for granted during the time when, as a very young man, I worked in the household of Robert Graves. But it was years of reading the knotted, allusive, reverberating poetry of David Jones that led me, to my surprise, to making these versions of the *Gododdin*. I think David Jones to be the most neglected, the least known great poet of the century, and as it happens one of the most pertinent to our time, but that is another subject. I have had passages of his writings in my head for years, and recently, rereading a translation of the *Gododdin*, it seemed to me suddenly that I could hear what the original must sound like because of the way it had been lovingly and gratefully echoed in the English of David Jones. After that, I returned to every English translation of the poem I could find, listening, and this selection and arrangement, these versions, are what I thought the poem might be like, or at least a suggestion of it.

—W. S. Merwin

The Story of the Lizard
Who Made a Habit of Having
His Wives for Dinner

At the edge of the river, hidden by the tall grass, a woman is reading.

Once upon a time, the book tells, there lived a man of very great substance. Everything belonged to him: the town of Lucanamarca, everything around it, the dry and the wet, the tamed and the wild, all that had memory, all that had oblivion.

But that lord of all things had no heir. Every day his wife offered a thousand prayers, begging for the blessing of a son, and every night she lit a thousand candles.

God was fed up with the demands of that persistent woman, who asked for what He had not wished to grant. Finally, either to avoid having to hear her voice any longer or from divine mercy, He performed the miracle. And joy descended on that household.

The child had a human face and the body of a lizard.

With time, he spoke, but he slithered along on his belly. The finest teachers from Ayacucho taught him to read, but his claws prevented him from writing.

At the age of eighteen, he asked for a wife.

His well-heeled father found him one, and the wedding was celebrated with great pomp in the priest's house.

The first night, the lizard threw himself on his wife and

devoured her. When the sun rose, in the marriage bed there was only the widower asleep, surrounded by small bones.

The lizard then demanded another wife, and there was another wedding and another devouring, and the glutton asked for yet another, and so on.

Fiancées were never lacking. In the households of the poor, there was always some spare girl.

• • •

His scaly belly lapped by river water, Dulcidio is taking his siesta.

Opening one eye, he sees her. She is reading. Never before in his life has he seen a woman wearing glasses.

Dulcidio pokes forward his long snout:

—*What are you reading?*

She lowers her book, looks at him calmly, and replies:

—*Legends.*

—*Legends?*

—*Ancient voices.*

—*What for?*

She shrugs her shoulders:

—*Company.*

This woman does not seem to be from the mountains, nor the jungle, nor the coast.

—*I know how to read too,* says Dulcidio.

She closes her book and turns her face away.

Before the woman disappears, Dulcidio manages to ask:

—*Where are you from?*

• • •

The following Sunday, when Dulcidio wakes from his siesta, she is there. Bookless, but wearing glasses.

Sitting on the sand, her feet hidden under many bright-colored skirts, she is very much there, rooted there. She casts her eye on the intruder.

Dulcidio plays all his cards. He raises a horny claw and waves it toward the blue mountains on the horizon.

—*Everything you see and don't see, it's all mine.*

She does not even glance at the vast expanse, and remains silent. A very silent silence.

The heir presses on. Many lambs, many Indians, all his to command. He is lord of all that expanse of earth and water and air, and also of the small strip of sand she sits on.

—*But you have my permission,* he assures her.

Tossing her long black tresses, she bows:

—*Thank you.*

Then the lizard adds that he is rich but humble, studious, a worker and above all a gentleman who wishes to make a home but has been doomed to widowerhood by the cruelties of fate.

She looks away. Lowering her head, she reflects on the situation.

Dulcidio hovers.

He whispers:

—*May I ask a favor of you?*

And he turns his side to her, offering his back.

—*Would you scratch my shoulder? I can't reach.*

She puts out her hand to touch the metallic scales, and exclaims:

—*It's like silk.*

Dulcidio stretches, closes his eyes, opens his mouth, stiffens his tail, and feels as he has never felt.

But when he turns his head, she is no longer there.

He looks for her, rushing full tilt across the field of tall grass, back and forth, on all sides. No trace of her. The woman has evaporated, as before.

● ● ●

The following Sunday, she does not come to the riverbank. Nor the next Sunday. Nor the following one.

● ● ●

Since he first saw her, he sees only her and nothing but her. The famous sleeper no longer sleeps, the glutton no longer eats.

Dulcidio's bedroom is no longer the pleasant sanctuary he took his rest in, watched over by his dead wives. Their photographs are all there, covering the walls from top to bottom, in heart-shaped frames garlanded with orange blossom; but Dulcidio, now condemned to solitude, lies slumped into his cushions and into despair. Doctors and medicine men come from all over, but can do nothing for the course of his fever and the collapse of everything else.

With his small battery radio, bought from a passing Turk, Dulcidio spends his nights and days sighing and listening to melodies long out of fashion. His parents, despairing, watch him pine away. He no longer asks for a wife, declaring *I'm hungry*. Now he pleads, *I am made a poor beggar for love*, and in a broken voice, and showing an alarming tendency to rhyme, he

> *pays painful homage to that certain She*
> *who stole his soul and his serenity.*

The whole populace sets out to find her. Searchers scour heaven and earth, but they do not even know the name of the vanished one, and no one has seen a woman wearing glasses in the neighborhood or beyond.

• • •

One Sunday afternoon, Dulcidio has a premonition. He gets up, in pain, and sets out painfully for the riverbank.

She is there.

In floods of tears, Dulcidio announces his love for the elusive and indifferent dreamgirl. He confesses that he *has died of thirst for the honeys of your mouth*, allows that *I don't deserve your disregard, my beautiful dove*, and showers her with compliments and caresses.

• • •

The wedding day arrives. Everyone is delighted, for the people have gone a long time without a fiesta, and Dulcidio is the only one there of the marrying kind. The priest gives him a good price, as a special client.

Guitar music engulfs the sweethearts, the harp and the violins sound in all their glory. A toast of everlasting love is raised to the happy pair, and rivers of punch flow under the great bouquets of flowers.

Dulcidio is sporting a new skin, pink on his shoulders and greenish blue on his prodigious tail.

• • •

Whena at last the two are alone and the hour of truth arrives, he declares to her:
—*I give you my heart, for you to tread on.*

She blows out the candle in a single breath, lets fall her wedding dress, spongy with lace, slowly removes her glasses, and tells him, *Don't be an asshole, knock off the bullshit*. With one tug, she unsheathes him like a sword, flings his skin on the floor, embraces his naked body, and sets him on fire.

Afterward Dulcidio sleeps deeply, curled up against this woman, and dreams for the first time in his life.

• • •

She eats him while he is still sleeping. She goes on consuming him in small bites, from head to tail, making little sound and chewing as gently as possible, taking care not to wake him, so that he will not carry away a bad impression.

Translated by Alastair Reid

The Prerogative of Lieder

Here comes the question
The weather the sun and its shadows
The unauthorized itch that was scratched
Here comes the question

Intuition devotion before or after
An answer a question an answer
Surely far below but on high
Dramatic steams cast in the sulks

Means more clouds
Space interviews the rhyme
And the entire weight decides not
With a shall instead of a will

Momentarily a cormorant is the distance
Knotted no lurking in quietude
The floral pot-shaped voice is autumn
Papered over with a spectacle of grieving wit

The customary harping immersed in a story
Truthful to remembering the asking where
And telling backwards from the poured hymn
Propped along the winter and profane

Climax Forest

A neat sunlit room
Filled with country arts—
Needlework and quilts.

A backwoods school of architecture:
Frame, a wide porch,
Deep eaves, a heavy,

Gently pitched roof—
Perhaps the house
Of a sawmill operator,

Predatory of the huge
Climax forest that once
Blanketed nearly all

Of North America, but
Living within its construct,
Flesh of its flesh.

It had been a beautiful
Day, and the beauty deepened.
In the orange light,

The long grasses at the edge
Of the garden seemed spun
From gold. The two

Had promised not to speak. She
Got into bed and like a vast
Nesting bird settled on him. It became

Like watching the river
For hours, watching
All the places it had wetted.

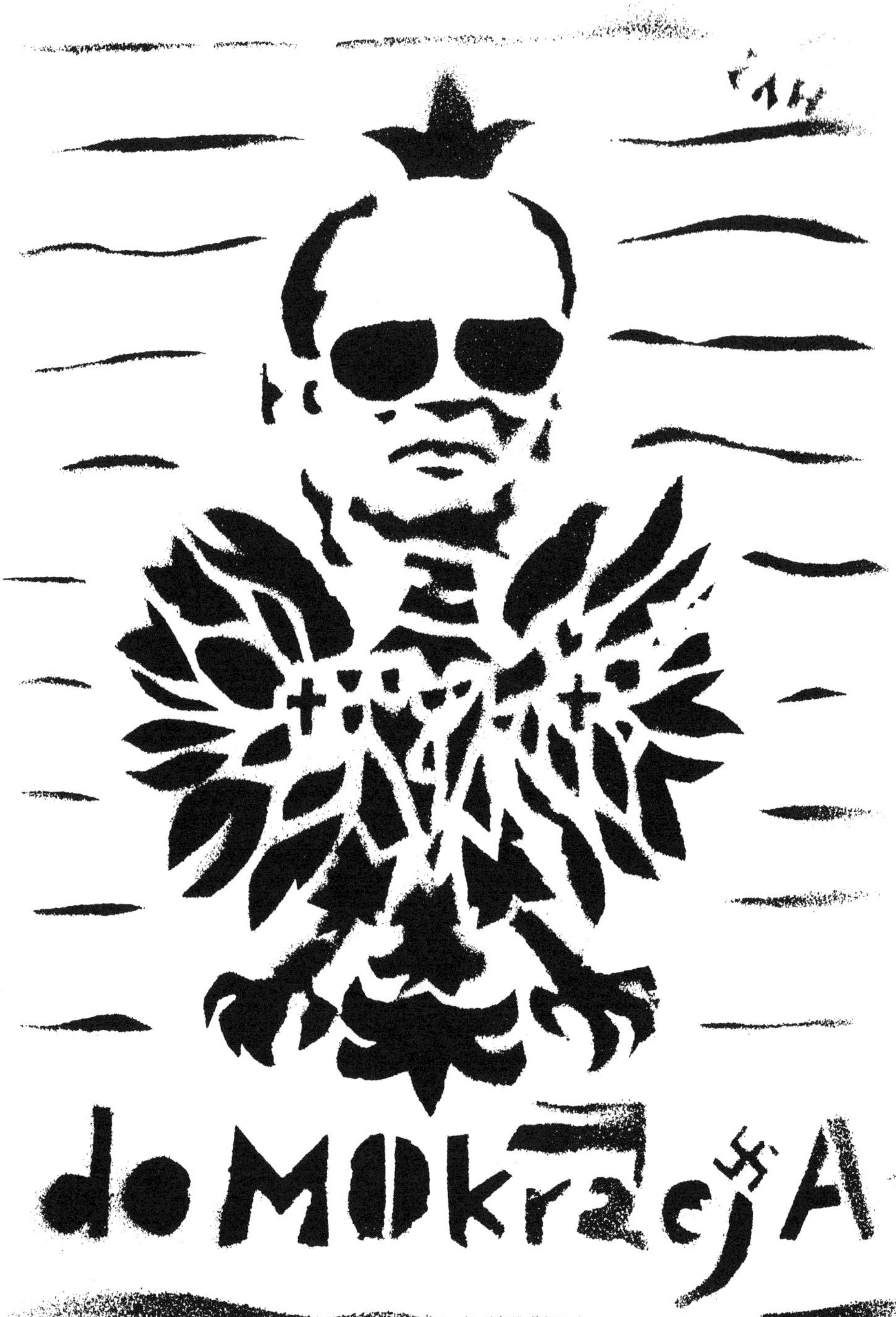
doMOkracjA

Swidnik:
A Polish Elegy

S omehow Poland is the saddest case. All over the former
Eastern bloc, the once-Communist economies have been
taking off. Or, rather, parts of them have. Capitalism has
been catching hold, and thousands, tens of thousands, even
hundreds of thousands of people have been able to grasp the
opportunity, to take advantage of it, to meld earlier opportunities
to new advantage. They are catching the wave. They will be
joining Europe, confidently striding into the twenty-first century.
Others, meanwhile—hundreds of thousands, millions of others—
feel themselves being left behind. And, generally speaking, the
ones being left behind are the industrial workers, the denizens
of those huge, superannuated Stalinist behemoths, the steel mills
and the textile plants and the tractor combines . . . Some of these
workers will make it, some will cross over, but many and perhaps
most will not. And if I say that Poland is the saddest case, this
is because it was Poland's industrial workers, more than anyone
else—*anywhere*—who brought about the whole transformation in
the first place.

• • •

A t a certain point during my most recent visit to Poland,
this past winter, I wanted to get out of Warsaw, simply to
get a feel for how things were going elsewhere. Almost

at random I chose to visit Swidnik, although actually I'd long wanted to go there. Legendary Swidnik! A small one-company town outside Lublin in far southeastern Poland, the one company a state aviation enterprise built up from scratch atop a plowed-under potato field by Poland's earliest Communist rulers, Swidnik had been one of the jewels of Stalinist planning and workers' culture, but had gradually become an ongoing torment to the heirs of those early rulers. The famous events of 1980, for example, began not, as is generally assumed, on August 14, when the workers in Gdansk's Lenin shipyard occupied their plant and proceeded to forge the Solidarity trade union, but six weeks earlier (in the immediate wake of a July 1 food price increase), when workers in Ursus, just outside Warsaw, and then throughout the Lublin area, occupied their plants. And the Lublin area strike, for its part, began in Swidnik.

When martial law was declared, seventeen months later, on December 13, 1981, one of the best-organized occupation strikes in Poland occurred at Swidnik. Although it was finally quashed by rampaging ZOMO shock troops, the citizens of Swidnik proved disconcertingly irrepressible, and all Poland thrilled to rumors of their continuing antics. That New Year's Eve, for example, the Swidnikites simply ignored the regime's strict curfew order and held a festive midnight party in the town's main square as if nothing had happened, popping champagne corks and making toasts all around, just as they had every year previously. By February, they had begun to demonstrate their disdain for the regime's nightly television news program by choosing precisely the hour of its broadcast to promenade ostentatiously, in the dead of winter, up and down the town's main allée—tens, hundreds, presently thousands of them, some of them pushing TV sets in baby prams. Infuriated, the regime reacted by clamping the earliest curfew in Poland on the town, whose residents in turn responded by parking their TVs on the narrow balconies of their apartments or in their opened windows, facing out, blasting the regime's irrelevancies into the indifferent night air. When the local authorities reacted by cutting the town's electricity at the appointed hour, the townspeople countered by placing lighted candles in their windows—keeping the entire town eerily aglow for precisely half an hour.

By May Day, when the local authorities decided to try to hold one of *their* traditional parades and began to erect the appropriate reviewing stands, the Swidnik workers let it be known that they'd march as ordered, but only with bare feet as they passed the tribunals. The authorities canceled the march and for good measure salted the main boulevards with fiberglass to prevent any unauthorized manifestations. As the American political scientist Roman Laba subsequently noted, "Swidnik passed into Polish workers' legend as the only town in the Soviet bloc not forced into, but forcibly prevented from, observing May Day." The next year, when the authorities tried once again, Swidnik's workers decided to let them have their little parade after all—meanwhile, they staged their own much better attended one, on a perpendicular side street.

Swidnik's branch of the clandestine Radio Solidarnosc was especially inventive, regularly managing to flicker into existence at the most inopportune moments. In February 1984, for example, as Polish television was broadcasting Yuri Andropov's state funeral in Moscow and the camera panned over the ancient visage of his wheezing successor, Konstantin Chernenko, the Swidnik gremlins suddenly jammed the audio portion of the feed with their own rendition of the old man's musings. "What's going on in Swidnik?" they had him muttering. *"What's going on in Swidnik?"* (And of course, that is precisely what he *was* thinking—or, if he wasn't, his soon-to-be heir Mikhail Gorbachev certainly was, and if not of Swidnik in particular then surely of Poland more generally. For all of the talk of Eastern Europe's eventual "liberation" by the clear-sighted Gorbachev, it's worth remembering that *perestroika* and *glasnost* came into being in the wake of the recent Polish experience; Gorbachev and his colleagues had been scared stiff by the spectacle of workers rising up against a workers' state and were frantically scrambling to fend off any similar upsurge within the Soviet Union.)

But all these high jinks were not without their cost. Under martial law, Swidnik's activists suffered an extraordinarily high rate of incarceration and an even higher rate of firing—a truly crushing fate in this town where there was, in effect, only one employer, or where, rather, the country's unique employer, the state, maintained but a single branch office. After a fifteen-minute warning strike in May 1982, management sacked 400 employees. Other actions provoked similar mass reprisals. For months fired workers would gather in the town's main square, milling together every day throughout their entire former workday, sustaining one another's hopes and defiance. Swidnik's Solidarity underground, meanwhile, was one of the country's most effective at addressing the material needs—food, shelter, clothing, medical services, and even recreation—of its victimized members. Throughout martial law, Solidarity lived in Swidnik.

So the first question was, what had survived Solidarity's triumph? The answer, which quickly became apparent the evening I took the half-hour drive from Lublin out to Swidnik, was: not much. Solidarity itself had fractured spectacularly, and the W.S.K. aviation plant was now laying off workers at a much fiercer clip than at any time during the worst days of martial law (the town's unemployment rate was already pushing beyond 15 percent) and stood a good chance of being shut down altogether. The plant's principal customer, the Soviet Union, was not only failing to place new orders but wasn't even paying for the aircraft it had already had delivered: in fact, that customer, for all intents and purposes, had ceased to exist. The quality of the plant's output, meanwhile, had so deteriorated in relation to world standards, particularly during the decade since martial law, that it wasn't clear if the plant could compete in any markets. The successive Solidarity regimes, beginning with Tadeusz Mazowiecki's in the fall of 1989, had failed to pursue any comprehensive restructuring program for Poland's aircraft industry (there are, all told, fourteen interlocking aviation plants throughout the country in situations roughly similar to Swidnik's), preferring instead generally to leave such restructuring to the eventual free play of market forces, with the result that in Swidnik—legendary Swidnik, the stalwart bastion of clandestine Solidarity—the party that received the highest number of votes in the most recent parliamentary election (October 1991) was the former Communists!

Mazowiecki's Unia party was represented in that election by Andrzej Sokolowski, the leader of the December 1981 strike and one of the heroes of the clandestine resistance, but he managed to garner only a thousand votes, coming in fifth behind the former Communists and three splinter oppositionist factions:

SPOJRZENIE W PRZESZŁOŚĆ
KRET

the Christian Nationalists, Centrum, and the KPN. "Somehow I imagined things would be different," Sokolowski conceded, when I spoke with him. "The most shocking thing for me, actually, has been the disappearance of the kind of social solidarity which during the eighties was not only the way we fought but what we fought for." He held Lech Walesa personally responsible for the movement's precipitous fracture. "There was no need to declare War at the Top when he did," Sokolowski insisted, referring to the slogan behind which Walesa had mobilized when he broke with his former ally Mazowiecki in 1990 and decided to push his own candidacy in early presidential elections. "There were a lot more important things to be worrying about at the time. But the truly dreadful thing was the way that that war filtered down to the bottom, here and everywhere else in Poland—how viciously longtime friendships and alliances and working relationships were smashed.

"At one point, for example, the Swidnik plant commission decided to create a special medal commemorating the tenth anniversary of Solidarity, to be granted to various activists who'd played prominent roles in the struggle—I, for instance, was given one— and I suggested that Wladek Frasyniuk would make an excellent candidate.* Back in May 1982, when we held our own fifteen-minute strike at the plant—which, by the way, was 100 percent effective—and 400 workers were fired the next day, Wroclaw Solidarity, all the way across the country, managed to send us a million zlotys, quite a sizable sum at the time, to help feed and house and care for those workers' families. I suggested that an award to Frasyniuk would allow us to show our retrospective gratitude for that gesture both to him and to the whole Wroclaw region, and everybody agreed. But by the time of the awards ceremony, several months later, War at the Top had broken out, and Frasyniuk, who was siding with Mazowiecki, was suddenly being cast as a terrible enemy. The rally was a horrible experience; Frasyniuk was

---

* Frasyniuk, the charismatic young leader of the Solidarity branch in the southwestern Polish city of Wroclaw, had electrified Poles with his exploits throughout the early days of martial law, when he not only managed to elude arrest for almost a year but did so while frequently popping up for impromptu rallies at factories all over his region.

rcpcatcdly shouted down by his hysterically hyped-up opponents. I don't even want to repeat what they said."

I asked him to anyway. He sighed. "'Treason!' they were shouting. 'Enemy!' 'Conspirer with Jews!' It was sickening. That's the day Solidarity died for me. I returned my own medal in protest.

"But that mood persisted, that level of anger and resentment and distrust. Do you know what really hurt during the last elections? To see activists for Centrum and the Christian Nationalists, my onetime friends and allies, rushing through the streets and ripping down my Unia posters while leaving the posters for the former Communists, right beside mine, entirely undisturbed. That's what's become of Solidarity here."

Sokolowski went on to talk about the way this anger and resentment went hand in hand with a kind of lethargy and paralysis, an inability to act on one's own or the plant's behalf, or to seize the initiative. People were simply overwhelmed by the enormity of what was happening to them. "What we should have been worrying about, for example, instead of War at the Top, was that developing fiasco with the Pope's helicopters."

I heard a lot about the Pope's helicopters while I was in Swidnik. In anticipation of the Pope's 1991 return pilgrimage to Poland, President Walesa's new, handpicked prime minister, Jan Krzysztof Bielecki, approved the ordering of twelve new helicopters from Bell-Textron, the American aircraft company. Swidnikites took this as a direct slap at their own cherished Sokol helicopter and, more to the point, as a crippling blow to the plant.

"The Bell affair was a scandal," Sokolowski continued, "And I even think some money must have changed hands. We ourselves didn't help matters any with all our infighting, and the workers' council changing managers every few months, one after another, and nobody bothering to lobby our deputies in the Sejm [the parliament] to prevent the sale or to make alliances with deputies from other regions where plants were going to be similarly affected. But mainly I think the culprits were the military and the police lobby. Granted, the Bell machine might have been more appropriate, perhaps slightly safer, for the Pope himself— but why did they need *twelve* Bell machines? Why couldn't they have rented one for the Pope and bought the others from us?

The Bell vehicle, with its single engine, doesn't even meet the minimum specifications for regular urban patrols: in Poland, helicopters flying over cities are required to have two engines, and our Sokol has them. The truth is, the police wanted those Bell vehicles so that they could strut like peacocks in their modern Western helicopters, and also so that they could train on Western equipment in preparation for the cushy jobs they all hope to land on retirement. But it was a terrible blow for us: that order by itself would have kept the plant going for a year at least, and the plant could have used the time and money to restructure—to refocus, for example, on the agro-aviation markets in Africa and Asia. Instead I see no perspective for the plant now, at least not in the short term. In the long term the Soviet situation will eventually stabilize, and they're likely to need our helicopters again. Only there's a good chance we won't be here anymore."

I subsequently had occasion to talk with Bielecki about Swidnik and the Pope's helicopters. "The folks in Swidnik wanted to become a superpower in the helicopter business," he said, a bit perturbed, it seemed, by the endless resurrection of this old story. "What they don't understand is that France and Germany have joined together to develop a new generation of helicopters. They believe they can compete with them, but they don't understand the economics of scale. Twelve helicopters, one hundred helicopters aren't enough. They imagine that, if they can just hold out, the Russians will come back on-line, and they will be able to offer them the same low-quality engines as they did under the artificial conditions of the past. But the Russians are going to want good engines." The place, he went on, required deep restructuring of the sort that the free market and not the government would have to impose. It was as simple—and as difficult—as that.

•   •   •

I had occasion to speak with other activists as well. Was what they'd got anything like what they'd imagined they'd been fighting for? "What we wanted both in 1980 and during martial law was freedom and independence," Urszula Radek, a stout, now-retired veteran of the plant and its struggles, told me

one evening as I sat with her, her husband, and her two sons in the
living room of their modest ground-floor apartment. "And despite
all the current problems, we are happy because we did achieve it.
I don't go to bed afraid that those guys may come barging in at
six in the morning. I sleep well. And even if I'm not feeding my
family as well as I used to—and I'm not—at least the stores are
full and it's a positive *pleasure* to shop, as it never was before. That
counts for something." Her voice trailed off, her mood darkening
visibly. "Still, we worry."

After a few moments, she continued. "Swidnik was a workers'
place. We built it. My father was here with the first crews in 1950.
I remember when it was all just four barracks in the mud. My
husband and I worked here, my sons . . . I have a right to call
it *my* factory. And a lot of the struggle here had to do with that
common sense of entitlement. We wanted, as everybody said, to
be subjects, not objects. It's strange: in the early days I think we
did feel like subjects. There was a tremendous optimism in the
fifties—all mixed up, to be sure, with all kinds of fearfulness and
suspicion. We are only eighty kilometers from the Soviet border
here; the plant was building components for MIG jet engines for the
Soviet military; we were obviously a key part of the Soviet military-
industrial complex; and the place was crawling with police and
soldiers—official, uniformed ones and many plainclothes, secret
types. Still, we had the feeling of accomplishment and constructive
momentum, a sense of building toward the future.

"Things began going seriously wrong in the seventies. We
heard of what happened up north in December 1970—I had
relatives in Gdansk—and that was of course very upsetting.* But at
first, Gierek was able to buy us off with his borrowed prosperity—

---

* Just before Christmas 1970, the one-time Communist reformer Wladyslaw
  Gomulka's increasingly rigid and petrified regime attempted an atrocious,
  across-the-board "restructuring" of the country's prices, lowering those for
  luxury goods while dramatically increasing the cost of bread and other
  necessities. The workers in the crucial Baltic port cities of Szczecin, Gdynia,
  and Gdansk exploded in fury, boiling out of their factories. The regime
  responded by suppressing these uprisings with terrible massacres. The inci-
  dents were immediately hushed up, but Gomulka soon fell nonetheless,
  replaced by another seeming reformist, Edward Gierek, whose regime
  likewise rigidified over the ensuing decade.

the TVs, the washing machines." She gestured about the room.*
"At the same time, though, the disparity between workers and
party members, the *nomenklatura* elite, was growing more and
more pronounced, this absurdity and immorality of certain people
being showered with privileges and perks simply because of their
party membership, while others who worked just as hard and
harder fell further and further behind. And that got much worse
after 1976, when the international banks shut the tap and Gierek's
little boomlet collapsed. By 1980 we were just fed up with being
treated like that, like . . . well, as I say, like objects."

Solidarity, the movement, the drama of the underground, had
been among the high points of Mrs. Radek's life, and she was
radiantly grateful when she spoke of them. And yet something
had clearly gone wrong once again. "I don't mean to be mean-
spirited," she said at one point. "Perhaps I am speaking too much,
but I speak of things that hurt: this business with the retirement
pensions, for example. Under the new law—and this is a Solidarity
government law—the monthly amount due any given person is
based on his or her best three consecutive years of salary any time
during the previous twelve. And that's terribly unfair. Because
what were those twelve years? Martial law, repression—years when
Communists or opportunists, those willing to join the martial law
replacement trade unions, for instance, all did wonderfully well in
material terms. It was easy to net a good salary if you were willing
to renounce all your ideals. But those who remained true to the
movement—who were fired in droves, or were regularly denied
overtime, or went years without any job advancement—they don't
have any 'three best years in a row.' So now the collaborators are
all getting nice fat pensions, while the rest of us . . ." Her voice
cracked.

I asked her whom she held responsible for this state of af-
fairs. Jacek Kuron, the veteran oppositionist and the first Solidarity government's minister of labor? "No, no," she said. "Not

---

* People wonder where the staggering $24 billion in foreign debt that Gierek
managed to build up in just those few short years of the early seventies all
went, and it's true that a lot of it was dissipated in extravagant corruption
and incompetence. But it's also true that you can still find a good portion
of that debt scattered about the country in the form of these clunky, boxy,
sixteen- and seventeen-year-old appliances.

him. Jacek is a good man. But the people under him, all the apparatchiks they didn't fire because they made it a principle that they weren't going to do so, well, those guys drafted the actual regulations, and they made sure to reward their own."

She was also resentful about the way the plant seemed to have been abandoned to its fate. "If the plant dies, this town will die. Can't they see that?" Why, I asked, couldn't people just pick up and move to somewhere with better prospects? She and her family all laughed bitterly. "Where? How? With what money? We spent fifteen years on a waiting list to get this apartment. Now the wait is, well, infinite: they aren't doing any more public housing. But even if there were housing available elsewhere—which there isn't—who would want to buy this apartment in this dying town so that we could afford to pay the rent somewhere else? That's the *whole* problem."

Back during the Solidarity period, when they'd all been struggling for independence and freedom, was it free markets and capitalist models they'd had in mind? "Actually not," Urszula Radek readily conceded. "We prized our solidarity. It was precious to us. Clearly we were imagining something more egalitarian."

"If we'd known then that this kind of raw capitalism was going to be our fate," her son interrupted, "we might have thought twice."

His mother winced. She couldn't imagine reconsidering the commitments of her glory years. Still, she agreed, social solidarity had withered. "During martial law we were so beautifully organized in our mutual assistance networks. Hundreds were fired, and we reached every one. Not one was forgotten. We found jobs with the outlying farmers, found doctors for the sick children. We had true solidarity. And that's gone. It completely evaporated here, like everywhere. Society became split up. Maybe it was because of the money, but with freedom all kinds of unpleasant instincts were freed up as well, and people started thinking only of themselves."

But wasn't that the idea? I asked. If you were going to have capitalism, solidarity was going to have to give way to competition, to a world of winners and losers.

"Too brutal," she said, and then repeated herself softly: "Too brutal, too brutal."

Did they think of themselves as subjects or objects these days?

"Objects," her husband, who'd sat silently, respectfully, in the corner the entire time, interjected almost before I could finish the question.

Mrs. Radek just shook her head. "What people think now is that they mustn't lose their jobs. That's their only concern. Fear is growing, people feel they don't have any influence over their own lives. People no longer talk in terms of subjects and objects; all they talk about is not losing their jobs."

Of course subjectivity is also common under capitalism, only it tends to be experienced individually, not socially. It is the domain of the struggling private entrepreneur. The trouble, as I was repeatedly told, is that the conditions for a fair struggle don't yet exist in Poland.

I spent a while talking with Alfred Bondos, another one of the heroes. Still quite a young man at the time, he'd become immensely popular during the original sixteen months of Solidarity, serving as an inspired activist deejay over the plant's public-address radio station. The night martial law was declared, MPs came storming up his apartment stairwell to arrest him, but he escaped by leaping four stories out a back window, badly breaking his leg in the process. Somehow he still managed to stagger over to the plant, where he helped Sokolowski lead the strike. After the strike's violent suppression, he managed to elude arrest for 370 days, 120 of which he spent hidden (and secretly provisioned) inside the plant itself! In 1983 he was finally captured and served half a year in jail. He'd remained an activist and had been elected to a term on the town council in the recent municipal elections. But, long since fired from his old position in the plant, he'd had to cobble together a series of alternative livelihoods, and recently he'd launched out on a private entrepreneurial venture of his own.

What kind? I asked.

"Worms," he replied. "California worms. Biohumus. I took my family's entire life savings, procured a 700-square-meter plot and a bunch of worms, and I'm trying to make a go of it composting organic fertilizer for the surrounding farmers."

How was it going?

"Not all that well, actually," he replied. "It's extremely difficult. The thing is, I watch worms now, and I see how it is with them.

They need certain things—not that many, but what they need, they
need. They need loam, oxygen, warmth. And it's the same with us,
we new small entrepreneurs. We are like the worms of the coming
capitalist order here in Poland, and we need certain things, too.
For instance, we need access to a certain minimal amount of credit. It's impossible for us to grow without it; it's like oxygen. Our
political leaders keep urging everyone to 'Leave those bankrupt
state enterprises, strike out on your own, show some initiative!'
Which is fine, only the banking system isn't there yet to sustain
that kind of development. Or not for everyone anyway. Certain
short-term credits are available, the kind that are useful for seat-
of-your-pants trade though not much else—two- or three-month
turnovers, that sort of thing. But if you need anything more long-
term, if you're trying to start a productive enterprise, there's no
credit available—that is, unless you know the right people.

"And *that's* the truly disgusting part," he continued. "Because
the thing you have to understand is that, in Swidnik, capitalism
didn't start in 1989; it started in 1988, when Rakowski,* reading
the writing on the wall, desperately began capitalizing the *nomenklatura.* For instance, the deputy mayor here in Swidnik, my main
enemy, the man who pursued me throughout my time in the
underground, was named director of the Swidnik bank, the only
bank in town. And the new Solidarity government never bothered
to challenge those appointments. So that when I go to the bank
now, my hat in my hand, seeking my few measly credits, whom do
you think I encounter there, smugly deciding my fate?"

"That's nonsense," replied Adam Michnik (the veteran dis-
sident activist, now editor of *Gazeta,* Warsaw's premier daily) a few
days later when I raised the example of Mr. Bondos in a discussion
of the alleged failure of the first few Solidarity governments to
overturn some of the more flagrant *nomenklatura* capitalizations.
"A Communist apparat who becomes the head of a bank ceases
to be a Communist at that very moment. It's true that if your
worm farmer's Solidarity friend had been named head of the
bank instead, it might have been easier for him, but only because
he'd have had a friend at the bank, not because of some higher
considerations of justice. This worm man's problem does disguise

* Mieczyslaw Rakowski, the last Communist prime minister.

a bigger, more real problem, however. Because where else were we going to find banking and other sorts of administrative talent, in the sorts of great numbers needed, if not from among the ranks of the former *nomenklatura?* Who else was going to have had the necessary experience?"

There *have* been exceptions, former oppositionist engineers and biologists and professors who've switched lives in midcareer to become, say, bankers. One of them, a former computer scientist named Wlodzimierz Grudzinski, who now heads a small, Labor-ministry-sponsored bank devoted specifically to small loans designed to spur employment growth, noted that part of Mr. Bondos's problem is that "It's simply easier for ordinary bankers to make one two-million-dollar loan than one hundred twenty-thousand-dollar ones. And it's also easier to lend money to a guy who wants to import ten tons of bananas from Berlin than to some other guy who wants to try his luck raising ten tons of California worms—because it's simply easier to evaluate the risk. Your worm guy doesn't need a different officer in charge of the Swidnik bank; he needs *three new banks* in Swidnik. And that takes time—time that, admittedly, he doesn't have. Poland today isn't so much changing its banking system as building a new one, almost from scratch. It's not a question of the chicken or the egg. It's 'No chicken, no egg—*you* go figure it out.'"

•   •   •

Not all former managers and *nomenklatura* types are so despised. In fact, in Swidnik I was repeatedly told that I should try to track down the aviation plant's former manager from the days of Solidarity. He'd been a fair man with a distinctive and powerful vision for the company. If only he'd been allowed to stay, instead of being fired shortly after the imposition of martial law, the plant might still have a fighting chance. Instead, not only had he been fired, he'd been forbidden to set foot in Swidnik again. He'd launched out on a new enterprise in Lublin, I was told, and my last day in the region I arranged to meet with him at the headquarters of his company there.

Not *his* company, Jan Czogala assured me with a smile as he ushered me into the compact, contemporary Western-style executive suite of Agrohansa, a spectacularly successful and burgeoning food-processing conglomerate, headquartered in a nondescript gray building on a dead-end side street near the edge of town.* He was a mere employee. The way he'd set the place up, his two daughters, one of whom, it turned out, I'd just met manning the assistant's desk right outside, were actually the ones nominally in charge. But yes, it was a successful enterprise, a company specializing in fruit and dairy processing that two years ago was already the second-largest private company in Poland, with the highest exports of any such enterprise. It now has over 2,000 employees. Czogala handed me his calling card, which was colorfully dappled with images of crisp, dew-freshened apples, cherries, and loganberries. The office, too, was crisp: dark wood paneling, white vertical window blinds, black leather chairs, a glass table. He was wearing a crisp black suit with a powder blue shirt; his face was soft and well scrubbed, with a high forehead and flowing, light brown hair; I guessed he was in his late fifties.

"I worked at Swidnik for twenty-six years," he informed me, as our conversation turned to his earlier career. "As I was *directed* to. I was, you see, a military man, a Polish army officer. I was assigned there, though as I gradually rose through the ranks at the plant—I began as a technical supervisor and presently shifted over to research and development—I was officially placed 'on leave.' But I was always a military man at heart."

He went on to describe some of the many innovations for which he'd been responsible and told me of the awards he'd received for, among other things, improving the efficiency of the MIG-2 jet. In part through licensing arrangements with General Motors and other Western firms, in part through innovations of his own, he'd made the plane 30 percent lighter and tripled the life expectancy of various engine components, doubling the plane's cost in the process—much to the annoyance of his Soviet overlords, who were regularly sending out investigative commis-

---

* After being fired in the wake of martial law, Sokolowski, the union activist, opened a modest vegetable stand in Lublin. Bondos was deep in worms. Czogala had started a food-processing conglomerate. It was as if Swidnik itself were reverting to its peasant roots.

sions to try to figure out what the hell was going on in Swidnik. But in the end they paid (at least in those days they still did), and Czogala continued to rise through the ranks—becoming head of the research division in 1972 and director of the entire plant in 1975.

He had to join the Communist party in conjunction with this last appointment, although he says he never had anything but disdain for the party. In part to upgrade the plant's technological profile, he systematically began reorienting the focus of Swidnik's activities from Soviet military contracts toward more Western clients—again much to the annoyance of the Soviets (Marshal Viktor Kulikov, the Red Army's chief of staff, himself paid an angry visit). By 1981, fully 25 percent of Swidnik's business was with Pratt & Whitney, Piper-Seneca, Airbus, and other such concerns. Had it not been for martial law, Czogala insists, that percentage would have continued to rise.

"I always had close contacts with the workers," he explained. "Swidnik was such a small town, you knew everything your neighbor was cooking for dinner, not to speak of all the secrets inside the plant. I lived in a small apartment and went to work at the same time as the workers." (At another point in our conversation, he said as many as 300 high party operatives in the Swidnik plant earned more than he did in his capacity as the place's director.) "So I wasn't surprised by the strike," he continued, referring to the crisis of July 1980. "By the late seventies, the whole country was increasingly tense. Prices were going up; living conditions were going down; the polarization in life circumstances between the elites and everybody else was becoming more and more pronounced; there was complete disarray at the top." He paused for a moment. "Just like now," he said, smiling. "An almost identical situation. If there were an organization like Solidarity now, it would be easy for them to take over. The country is longing for an organized counterforce. The difference is that then it was able to invent one."

That diffuse sense of national dissatisfaction began to focus considerably on July 1, 1980, Czogala recalled, when an arbitrary set of steep new food price increases was introduced. "I woke up feeling, 'This is it, it's going to happen any day now.' And sure enough, just a few days later, we had our cutlet incident."

The incident with the cutlet is one of the most famous way stations on the road to Solidarity. A worker in a factory canteen grabbed a pork chop and, cursing in disgust—"Look at this thing! Not only is it more expensive than before, *it's smaller!*"—proceeded to march around the factory yard, gathering an ever-larger crowd behind him. And it happened in Swidnik, outside Lublin, on July 9, 1980.

"Within a few hours, several thousand workers were angrily milling around in the plaza outside the administration building," Czogala recalls. "As I say, I'd been expecting something like this. I immediately gave orders to have loudspeakers installed, then took a microphone in hand and urged the people to stay inside the factory's perimeters, not to go marching off to burn down the party headquarters or anything like that." He was terrified of another incident like the 1970 Gdansk massacre. He invited any individual worker to come up and address the crowd. "But unfortunately the first several stammered in their excitement and were completely incoherent." Eventually he took back the mike and explained that the thing they were going to have to do at this point was elect themselves a strike committee and come up with some *demands;* they'd all reconvene in a few hours, but he needed some demands to pass on up the chain of command. As much as anyone else—and everyone agrees about this—the director at Swidnik helped organize the strike there.

The next few hours were fraught with tension. This, of course, was before the Lenin shipyard went out in Gdansk. Swidnik was standing alone in its defiance: a factory less than eighty kilometers from the Soviet border—and not just any factory, but one of the key installations of the Soviet military-industrial system. Czogala got on the phone to Warsaw and was told that a squadron of Polish military helicopters was already en route to pacify the situation. Czogala, fearing a bloodbath (Swidnik, as a military plant, was well stocked internally with machine guns and other weaponry, and it wasn't at all clear who currently controlled this arsenal), managed to convince the Warsaw authorities to hold back the helicopters for a while. The strike committee, after several delays, came back with 111 demands—both political and economic, though not yet including the call for independent, free trade unions (a demand that would surface only in Gdansk)—and the Swidnik strikers dug in for the long haul. The next day, a high government minister arrived from Warsaw and attempted to address the crowd. "He was hooted down, and I had to take him out by the back door. He was terrified." Warsaw, no doubt under increasing pressure from Moscow, put more and more pressure on Czogala: the helicopter squadron continued to idle at an airfield halfway to Swidnik.

Presently, Czogala recalls, he met with the plant's strike committee and tried to convey to them the growing perils of the situation. "Look," he recalls telling them, "you guys can keep this strike up for a few more days, but after that you're really going to have to call it off; otherwise we're going to have a bloodbath here. But why don't you get in touch with the auto plant or the railworkers* in Lublin, so that just as you call off your strike they can be starting up their own." Thus, according to Czogala, did Poland's famous "rolling strike" of the summer of 1980 first come into being. Not only did Swidnik's strike spread to Lublin, but from there it kept rolling on from one region to the next until, five weeks later, on August 14, it finally reached the Lenin shipyards in Gdansk. "Oh yes," he advised his workers, "And you really should set up some kind of interfactory strike committee."

The sixteen months of Solidarity were exhilarating ones for Czogala personally, and beyond that they constituted a highly productive period for the plant. In fact, the growing chaos notwithstanding, 1981 was the most productive year in Swidnik's history—even though it was cut short on December 13. On December 8, Swidnik's workers voted to banish the Communist party organization from the plant, and Czogala went along with that decision. By the end of the week, however, Czogala was receiving intimations that something was afoot: he and the Solidarity leaders inside the plant kept each other abreast of developments, and it was partly due to their coordination that workers were able to occupy their key facility before the martial law authorities could secure it. By 5:15 A.M. that Sunday morning, there were already 600 people inside the plant (Jaruzelski's grave televised announcement of martial law only began to be broadcast at 6:00 A.M.), and by 7:00, when the military helicopters came

---

* Lublin was a key rail junction connecting the Soviet Union with points west, including, ultimately, East Germany.

swooping in overhead, there were already 2,000 workers holding down the fort, Czogala among them.

A few hours later, as Czogala and the strike leaders, including Bondos and Sokolowski, were meeting to draft their common strike demands (the suspension of martial law, the release of all prisoners, and the removal of all the military forces surrounding the plant), Czogala was handed a set of written orders from the martial law commander in charge of the Lublin district, officially remilitarizing him and ordering him to abandon the premises forthwith. "I simply informed my colleagues that I was going to ignore this order: I'd been in Swidnik for twenty-six years, and I fully intended to stay with my crew," Czogala recalls. (This gesture, which I subsequently had confirmed by Sokolowski, was arguably among the most heroic made that day: as a military man, Czogala was consciously risking both court-martial and execution.) "The strike leaders were so astonished that they arrested me on the spot. 'For your own good' is how they put it." Czogala got up and rifled through a filing cabinet over in the corner, returning with a somewhat tattered sheet of paper. "They made it official with this document, you see"—the typed document, bearing several flourishing signatures at the bottom like some makeshift Declaration of Independence, officially records the events of the week and concludes with the phrase "In order to prevent an increase in tensions due to the uncontrolled activities of the director, we, the strike committee, decided to place him under the supervised protection of the workers"—"which they gave me just before the ZOMOs stormed the plant. And this piece of paper probably saved my life."

By evening, 5,000 workers had joined the plant's occupation, and the military had the place completely ringed. Many workers wanted to arm themselves for the upcoming confrontation, but Czogala strenuously urged nonviolence. Two nights later, when the ZOMOs finally stormed the gates, they encountered no armed resistance. "We were all holding hands," Czogala recalls, "the crew and I, as they beat us. At a certain moment, two guys came over and, singling me out, placed me under arrest and dragged me away in a police car. I had no idea what fate awaited me, except I knew that, as an officer, I was in serious trouble."

He was held in prison until the day before Christmas when,

after being told that his case remained under active review, he was given a brief furlough and ordered to report to Warsaw. There he met with the vice-minister of defense, General Jan Nowak, who summarily relieved him of his military commission (he'd been officially fired as head of Swidnik even before the ZOMOs invaded), commenting contemptuously, "Czogala, you were a good manager but a bad politician." (Recently Czogala got some soft revenge in this regard. He published an open letter to this general in an independent Lublin newspaper that he helps to sponsor. "Minister Nowak," his letter began, "you were both a bad politician and a bad administrator.") Czogala was given to understand that Jaruzelski and other members of the general staff were particularly furious with him and were intending serious and exemplary punishment. Before he could be returned to prison, some doctor friends helped him stage a phony heart attack and ordered him into the intensive care unit at their hospital, thereby shielding him for the next several months from any military inquisitors. Tensions were running so high, however, that a few weeks later Czogala suffered a *real* heart attack, after which it became somewhat easier for the doctors to continue their subterfuge. Gradually tempers cooled, the process was prolonged and obfuscated, and Czogala's precious piece of paper safeguarded him through a few important hearings, until finally he was included in one of the general amnesties. But he was resettled in Lublin and sternly warned that he was never to have contact with Swidnik—damn Swidnik!—ever again.

As the years passed, he embarked on a series of private business initiatives, most of them (including the founding of Agrohansa three and a half years ago) joint ventures with some of the German industrialists and financiers he'd already been doing business with in his prior incarnation. (Germans are by far the greatest foreign investors in Poland.) Czogala is obviously a born manager, an artist of the material world. At one point he unscrolled, with great pride, an organizational chart of his new company (with a slot labeled "Agrohansa Holding Company" hovering at the top and lines radiating neatly and compactly down to other boxes labeled "Agrohansa Lublin," "Agrohansa Rzeszow," "Agrohansa Hamburg," "Agrohansa Tunisia," and so forth): it looked for all the world like the design specifications for a sophisticated new helicopter.

And it suddenly became clear to me how much Swidnik had lost in losing a manager of Czogala's caliber. When I tried to edge our conversation in that direction, Czogala discounted his own importance. "But," he went on, "the consequences of martial law torment the Swidnik plant to this day. They fired hundreds of people, including almost all the important division managers, all the people with contacts throughout the world. There has been no investment in capital for ten years. Ten years ago, Swidnik was an extremely modern plant—the Sokol helicopter was not bad for its time, for fourteen years ago. During my tenure, we sold over a hundred of them to the West. But the martial law authorities broke all that. For the past ten years the plant has been governed by a bunch of idiots with red passports, and they simply destroyed the place."

(Czogala's comments reminded me of some similar ones made a few days earlier by Halina Bortnowska, a leading Solidarity theorist and lay Catholic activist, back in Warsaw. "Nowadays," she told me, "it's become fashionable to suggest that, who knows, maybe martial law was all for the best. Even the Cardinal tries to justify it, and everybody's forgiving. But I wonder. Before it happened, I worried that if this grasp of ours was broken, it would have epochal implications, would break us forever. Then it happened, and we resisted, and with our resistance I began to hope that maybe I'd been wrong. But now I look back, and I begin to doubt it. The resistance was too small. People suffered more than we knew. Something essential *was* broken. I mean, we're the same people whom it was once possible to mobilize ten million strong, and now everyone is atomized, we're small particles swirling in a whirlpool, without coherence. The elites were perhaps blinded to this reality by their small resistances, but we're all paying for the trauma now. More happened then than we have yet realized.")

Czogala's thoughts drifted to the persistent and pervasive corruption among both those old red-passport elites and the new *nomenklatura* and to the difficulties of doing honest business in such an environment. "My responsibility is to take care of my workers, and I haven't had to fire a single one, except for alcohol or theft. I could have made millions illegally, and I have to compete against people who do. A while back I was bidding for a small company against the so-called Art B boys. Maybe you've heard

of them: incredibly successful young entrepreneurs, who, sure enough, turned out to be engaged in all kinds of shady dealings. There was no way I could match their offer, but I told the people at this company, 'Friends, Rockefeller made his money quickly but he was the only one. Decent people should work hard and long. Such big money in one year cannot be clean. I only know how to make decent money and preserve your jobs.' They ended up going with Art B, naturally, and now Art B has gone bankrupt, the boys have absconded with the money, and these people are left in the lurch. Here in Lublin, there's a company we compete with that employs all the former party secretaries; it's run by a mysterious American, actually a former Soviet citizen, named David Bogatin, who also runs the main private bank here in Lublin. Who knows where his money comes from—it all seems pretty fishy to me—but they regularly undercut our prices at every turn. Their people keep producing whatever we set out to produce—frozen fruit, yogurt, candy—for less. It's clear they've corrupted some of my foreign-trade employees. And my people are always saying, 'Look, why not go to the police?' I tell them this is a free market, we've just got to do better than Bogatin's people, our wits are our only defense, no police will help us. But it's exasperating. And I know that others have fallen by the wayside because of this sort of competition."*

"My goal these days," Czogala continued, "is to produce as much as possible—well and cheaply. To try to make small but consistent profits in this very difficult environment. And in fact we're beginning to produce large quantities of quality products,

---

* Czogala's intuition about Bogatin proved correct. In the weeks immediately following our conversation, the Warsaw daily *Gazeta*—notably, not the Lublin police or the state authorities—revealed that Bogatin was in fact a convicted gangster who, back in New York, had been found guilty, along with a leading captain in the Colombo crime family, of operating a so-called daisy chain gasoline bootlegging operation that bilked federal and state governments of millions of dollars in taxes. In March 1987, he was found guilty of filing false tax returns; shortly after, he skipped bail while awaiting an appeal of his sentence. Bogatin is a Russian Jew, and his supporters initially accused *Gazeta* of flagrant anti-Semitism, a sweet change of pace for the editors there, many of whom are themselves Jewish and regularly subject to anti-Semitic slurs. But the news eventually provoked a run on Bogatin's bank, Poland's largest such private institution, and led to a new financial crisis for the country's already-strapped treasury. Bogatin himself, meanwhile, was extradited back to the United States in the spring of 1992.

attractively packaged, the sort of things that just a few months back were still being imported: milk, yogurt, ice cream. We're beginning to recapture that market. My responsibility as a manager is the same as it was back in my Swidnik days, to provide the best possible living standards for my crew but also to keep in perspective the requirements of the enterprise as a whole. I remember how I used to have to say to my Swidnik colleagues, 'Instead of pay increases for you, we should invest today so that your children will be assured jobs.' And we sacrificed accordingly. It's one of the great sorrows of my life that everything that is happening there today contradicts the spirit of those efforts and those promises."

I asked him about Swidnik's prospects and those of the rest of Poland's state industrial base, and in particular about the policies of the successive Solidarity governments in this regard.

"I feel profoundly for my old colleagues at Swidnik, and I try to help in small ways. I could easily order freezer compartments abroad, but instead I've tried to set up a small assembly line in Swidnik in a corner of the old plant. This is not merely a matter of altruism; these are my customers, and what good is it going to do me if I can get cheaper freezer compartments abroad, but Polish consumers can't afford to buy the products I put in them? It's in my interests to see that people are gainfully employed. But there's relatively little that I, as an individual entrepreneur, can do, and the challenges at a place like Swidnik are enormous.

"I myself favor free markets, free competition," he continued. "I believe that competition frees energy and releases inventiveness and brings the best to the top. But in the beginning, in a situation like ours, the state can't just throw up its hands and claim that it doesn't care, that it's everybody for themselves. It's like throwing a baby into a lake and expecting it to swim. I liked Balcerowicz* and I esteemed him highly, but we needed a second Balcerowicz, one who'd have done for production and industrial policy and

* Leszak Balcerowicz, the finance minister in the first several Solidarity governments, was the author of the shock-transition plan that both stemmed hyperinflation and provoked a serious recession. A darling of the IMF, the World Bank, and various Western governments and advisors, he was replaced after the October 1992 parliamentary elections, though the fundamentals of his program were largely retained.

directed, planned conversion what the first one was doing for the wider fiscal and monetary policies. Our terrible recession, it seems to me, was not so much caused by the actions of the first as by the lack of the second. And that lack has had a devastating impact on Swidnik and other places. The whole thing's a tragedy."

My time in Lublin was drawing to a close, and Czogala offered to have his driver take me back to the train station. Downstairs, as we left the building, the morning fog had lifted, and I was able to see past two or three houses to the side street's dead end, beyond which the terrain opened out on a marshlike depression, a vast scrabbly hollow, with acres and acres of dead, tufted straw peeking out amidst the muddy snow, and bleak, gnarled guard towers overlooking the scene every few dozen yards. The whole landscape resembled nothing so much as an Anselm Kiefer painting.

What's *that?* I asked the driver.

"Majdanek," he replied laconically.

History has a way of ambushing you like that every once in a while in Poland, almost lacerating you with its ironies. It turns out that the Majdanek death camp—unlike, say, its counterpart in Auschwitz, several dozen kilometers outside Krakow—was located cheek by jowl with the city it was in part designed to bleed and drain. The gash has been left there, untouched, an open wound, surrounded by the busy ongoingness of life—and in this instance, it occurred to me, by Mr. Czogala's admirably thriving Polish-German joint venture.

•　•　•

Coda:

On the train back to Warsaw, as I pondered the collapse of Solidarity and the seemingly inevitable and profoundly unfair supersession of the very workers—in Swidnik and elsewhere—who'd brought about the revolution in the first place, I happened to be reading Roman Laba's provocative revisionist tract, *The Roots of Solidarity.** Laba published his book last year in mutually acknowledged tandem with a book by his fellow heretic, Lawrence

---

* Princeton University Press, 1991.

Goodwyn, the distinguished historian previously known for his studies of American populism. Goodwyn's book, *Breaking the Barrier,** is more detailed but also a good deal more angrily polemical in tone—at times dismayingly so. But both books lay out a novel thesis that distinctly refutes much of the received wisdom regarding the origins of Solidarity. It seems to me that, in true heretical fashion, both authors go overboard (Laba somewhat less so): it is after all the nature of heretics to uncover long-suppressed aspects of the truth and then, in their enthusiasm, to raise those aspects to the level of The Whole Truth, so that their error ends up being not so much one of verity as of proportion. But Laba's book still seems uncannily prescient.

According to the standard account, the rise of Solidarity came as the outcome of a long-deferred unification of oppositionist worker and intelligentsia movements. The intelligentsia struck in 1968 but were largely ignored and even disdained by the workers; two years later, when the workers rose up and called on the intelligentsia for support, the latter, still nursing their wounds from two years before, demurred; and it was only after 1976, when a worker uprising was again quashed and certain members of the intelligentsia at last rose to the defense of the repressed worker activists (through the creation of KOR, the Workers Defense Committee, by such activists as Jacek Kuron, Adam Michnik, Bronislaw Geremek, Jan Jozef Lipski, Henryk Wujec, and Jan Litynski), that the stage was finally set for the kind of united challenge—the intelligentsia providing its theoretical and practical expertise, the workers their brute strength and strategic positioning—that would eventually bear fruit in 1980 with the emergence of Solidarity.

This view is very much that of the Polish intelligentsia and, according to Laba and Goodwyn, vastly overestimates the significance of that intelligentsia's contribution. Neither Laba nor Goodwyn minimizes the heroic courage of many of these intellectual activists, particularly in the period before 1980, but they do take issue with the latter's appraisal of their ultimate role. The intelligentsia's view has become the received version of

---

* Oxford University Press, 1991.

events because of what Laba calls "the problem of gatekeepers": Westerners get their view of developments primarily from the accounts of their counterparts elsewhere. The Poles whom Western journalists, professors, and other intellectuals end up talking with are mainly journalists, professors, interpreters, and the like.

Laba and Goodwyn argue that, in fact, the Polish workers had themselves achieved all of the major conceptual and tactical breakthroughs on their own, long before the intellectuals arrived on the scene. They themselves had already grasped the importance of occupying their factories and forcing the regime to come to them, rather than spilling out onto the streets where they could be massacred; the crucial significance of the demand for independent trade unions, rather than merely for pay increases or other sorts of concessions; and so forth. The intellectual advisors regularly lagged behind the curve at all the key moments of the summer of 1980, and the tension between the radical democratic impulses of Polish workers and the more conventional elitist proclivities of Polish intellectuals bedeviled the movement throughout the sixteen months of its aboveground existence.

As I say, I think Laba and Goodwyn exaggerate and over-schematize matters somewhat: for one thing, what is one to make of the role of a loose-cannon army officer, on leave and heading a key military-industrial plant, who may actually have been the one who invented the rolling strike and the interfactory strike committee? But their formulations are suggestive, especially in light of what happened nine years later, when the intellectual elites assumed command of the oppositionist side, first in the roundtable negotiations, and presently in the first two Solidarity governments as well, to a certain extent marginalizing the workers and their contribution.

Roger Boyes, the Eastern European correspondent for the *Times* of London, recently published an article* in which he discusses the class of young technocratic reformers, journalists, and other members of the intelligentsia that came into being with the events of 1956 and further coalesced in opposition to the anti-Semitic purges of 1968—in particular, the group centered

* The *Warsaw Voice*, November 17, 1991.

around the relatively progressive Communist weekly *Polityka*. He cites a photograph taken in 1978 outside the lakeside dacha of that journal's editor, Mieczyslaw Rakowski (who would later become the last Communist prime minister of Poland), that shows the weekly's far-flung staff all lounging about in celebration of the twentieth anniversary of Mr. Rakowski's editorial tenure. I, too, have long marveled at that photograph, because it displays a group of people, half of whom would, within the next three years, find themselves arresting the other half.* Several of those pictured—Rakowski himself, Jerzy Urban, Wieslaw Gornicki, Daniel Passent—became key figures in or apologists for the martial law government, while several others—Stefan Bratkowski, Dariusz Fikus, Ryszard Kapuscinski, Wanda Falkowska, Hanna Krall, Andrzej Wroblewski—went on to play highly visible roles in the Solidarity-allied opposition.

Boyes, however, points out how, in the wider arc of time, the split was less definitive than it might at first have appeared. The oppositionist wing of this group proved elastic enough to absorb a few Solidarity worker-leaders (such as Zbigniew Bujak and Wladyslaw Frasyniuk) and of course came to make common cause with such "professional dissidents" as Jacek Kuron and Adam Michnik, as well as with various "nonfanatical members" of the Catholic intelligentsia. And indeed it is that wider group, "that political nucleus," that has been running the country since 1989. But the thing to understand was that it still had clear and powerful "connections with the group that had just surrendered power," that is, with the other people in the photograph. "There is nothing shameful about any of this," Boyes insists. "Indeed, this closeness made the February 1989 roundtable discussions possible. To the West it seemed as if communist jailers were talking to former political prisoners, but the relationship was more complex. The 'them' and 'us' of the 1980s, the communists versus the dissidents, was a false dichotomy."

This dovetails nicely with Laba and Goodwyn's argument, and it helps to explain the seeming abandonment of Poland's working

---

* See my annotation of the photo, "Poland's Best and Brightest," in *Harper's* magazine, December 1985, reprinted in the collection of *Harper's* annotations, *What's Going on Here?* (Delta, 1991).

class and, in turn, the latter's surly (if somewhat inchoate) revenge during the 1991 parliamentary elections. "Suddenly, it emerges that this cozy class is too narrow and too limited in its ambitions to carry Poland through to the next stage," Boyes notes. "It has not been able to convince Poles to accept the sustained hardship of a Thatcherite program. That is what Mr. Walesa meant [during the War at the Top] . . . when he started to talk of the arrogance of the intellectuals and to pit Gdansk, the workers' citadel, against Warsaw." (Again, the actual situation is considerably more subtle and convoluted than this schema suggests. Lately, for example, Walesa himself endeavored to reunite with his erstwhile foes— Michnik, Geremek, and the others—in opposition to such former allies as the prime minister Jan Olszewski, who was defeated in the recent elections, and his lieutenants Zdzislaw Najder and Jaroslaw Kaczynski.)

But Laba's book adds another aspect to this picture, for a deeply tragic subtext runs through his argument. Yes, it was the workers who made all this happen, yes it was they (and not the intellectuals) who made the great tactical and programmatic leaps—but their cause was foredoomed to fail.

Most theories of history see revolutions as generated by rising classes elbowing their way onto the world stage, but Laba, borrowing a notion from Barrington Moore, suggests instead that "it is not rising classes that generate revolutionary upheavals, but dying classes." It is tempting, he continues, "to identify the industrial proletariat in Soviet systems as a dying class on the point of becoming revolutionary, just as small artisans and peasants became revolutionary in the nineteenth and twentieth centuries." Laba goes on to argue that the Soviet-type regimes (including Poland, the rest of Eastern Europe, and China) time and again "legitimated themselves by building nineteenth-century economies and proletariats." While they treated their proletariats materially better (in terms of universal education, health care, and job security) than did, say, their counterparts in early-nineteenth-century England, this couldn't compensate for the fact that their project was anachronistic in its very essence, a fact that became all the more evident when the realities of the world (the evolving shape of the global market, the exigencies of the security confrontation) "forced them to face technological change while saddled with antiquarian tools." They were, he concludes, "rigidified Leninist states entangled with oversized and outdated working classes."

On my return to America, I telephoned Laba to ask him about what I took to be the profoundly tragic cast in his formulation, and he did not shy away from my characterization. He referred to the work of the Stanford economist Ronald McKinnon, who has recently formulated a perversely ironical "law of the subtraction of value." "From time immemorial," Laba explained, "from before the Stone Age, labor involved adding value to the finished product. The Soviet-type economy was the first in which you put more value in and got less out. For instance, in a Soviet-style steel mill, such as Poland's Nowà Huta, you'd put in ore, labor, all these things of great value, and what came out the other end, typically, was this totally useless crap. The Law of the *Subtraction* of Value. A paradoxical corollary to the law is that the more such a society is forced to expand, the more likely it is to implode. And that's what happened in Poland."

The agents of the implosion were the workers themselves, but their fate was far from joyous.

"Yes," Laba agreed. "It's sad, profoundly sad."

Note on Stencils

In the late eighties, stencils developed into the major form of graffiti in Poland. The artists—usually teenagers with an artistic background—chose to remain anonymous or to hide behind the mask of a pseudonym. In big cities and small towns across the country, images would appear on the walls of public places; to some extent they still do. Underpasses were favorite locations. Some of these places have been turned by the artists into "stencil galleries," where the ever-growing number of images on the walls creates a sort of street journal.

The stencilmakers are primarily identified or associated with anarchist, antitotalitarian, punk, vegetarian, and nonviolent communities or networks. But some of them are skinheads and fascists, while others are involved in the street-advertising of artistic events. During the 1990 presidential elections, a large part of the underground stencil network organized a mean anti-Walesa campaign. Recently stencils have also been used for commercial campaigns, such as to advertise one of the new daily papers, *Obserwator*.

Stencils, by allowing artists easily to multiply their images and messages, permit a free and independent flow of information and an affirmation of the attitudes of the new, non-Solidarity generation. These artists have taken the aesthetics and language of the totalitarian society and, by rearranging its signs, have made their own use of them, finding new ways to describe the world and mark fresh paths to beauty.

—Piotr Bikont

p. 192   Artist: "Iah" (from "Jan"). Polish national emblem, the crowned eagle (deprived of its crown by the Communists), with the head of General Jaruzelski.

p. 197   Artist: "Kret" (Mole). Two Soviet soldiers "looking back into the past."

p. 202   Artist: "Bekon" (Bacon). "B. I. Uljanow" (Lenin) with a mohawk.

p. 209   Artist: "Ski" (common ending of Polish surnames). Soviet soldier conquering the world.

p. 216   Artist: anonymous. "New proletariat": a topless woman's body.

p. 223   Artist: anonymous. Man displaying his bare bottom.

Sherrie Levine
Untitled (After Duchamp: Chessboards) #4, 1989
Tempera on wood in glass and wood vitrine
24¼ x 24¼ x 69 in.

E ach cover of *Grand Street* features an actual-size detail of a chosen artwork. The entire work is reproduced above. An enlarged detail from the same work appears on the title page. A portfolio of related work by Sherrie Levine begins on page 81.

Ulla Åberg is the chief dramaturge at the Royal Dramatic Theatre, Stockholm, where she has worked on plays by Shakespeare, Strindberg, and O'Neill, among others.

Aneirin, to whom the *Gododdin* is attributed, wrote (if he existed) in the sixth century. For more information, see W. S. Merwin's note following the poem.

Félix de Azúa was born in Barcelona in 1944, and received his doctorate in philosophy from the university there. He has taught at Oxford and at San Sebastián in Spain. He is currently Professor of the Philosophy of Art at the School of Architecture in Barcelona. His books include a collection of poems, three volumes of essays, and four novels, and have been translated into many languages.

Burlin Barr's poems have recently appeared in *Northwest Review.* He was born in Waxahachie, Texas, and now lives in Ithaca, New York.

J. Borges was born in 1935 in the village of Bezerros, Pernambuco, Brazil, where he still lives. He is an engraver of woodcuts, a poet, and a printer. He is the leading artist in the popular northeastern Brazilian tradition of *cordel:* small pamphlets that recount, in verse and images, news of the region and of the world, old legends and stories, etc.; they are sold in the markets of each town.

Mel Chin was born in Houston and now lives and works in New York City. A recent traveling exhibition of his sculpture was organized by the Walker Art Center in Minneapolis; he has also had solo exhibitions at the Frumkin-Adams Gallery in New York and the Hirshhorn Museum in Washington.

Yiorgos Chouliaras is known in Greece as the author of several books of poems, among them *The Other Tongue* and *The Treasure of the Balkans.* A new book, *Fast-Food Classics,* has just been published in Athens. Chouliaras lives in New York City.

Carol and **Thomas Christensen**'s translations from Spanish include books by Julio Cortázar, Carlos Fuentes, and Alejo Carpentier. Forthcoming this year are translations of novels by Manuel Vázquez

Montalbán and Laura Esquivel and an anthology, *The Discovery of America and Other Myths: A New World Reader.* He is executive editor of Mercury House; she is a freelance editor and book reviewer. They live in the San Francisco Bay Area.

Lo Dagerman, the daughter of Stig Dagerman and the Swedish film and stage actress Anita Björk, was born in Stockholm in 1951. She now works as a transportation consultant in Bethesda, Maryland, where she lives with her husband and their two children.

Stig Dagerman was born in Alvkarleby, Sweden, in 1923. Considered one of Sweden's most important twentieth-century authors, he wrote four novels, a collection of short stories, two books of essays, several full-length plays, and a number of shorter prose works before his prolific career was cut short by his death in 1954.

Ray DiPalma's recent books include *Metropolitan Corridor* (Zasterle, 1992) and *Mock Fandango* (Sun & Moon, 1991). A video based on his prose work *January Zero* (Coffee House Press, 1984) was made last year in France.

A. J. Dunning is head of the Department of Cardiology at the University of Amsterdam. He has been writing for more than twenty years about medicine and society. He lives with his wife, children, "and books" in the Dutch countryside.

Mark Flood is Professor of Fine Arts at the University of Texas, Dallas.

Eduardo Galeano was born in Montevideo, Uruguay, in 1940. His trilogy *Memory of Fire* (Pantheon) won the American Book Award in 1989. He is also the author of *Open Views of Latin America* and *Days and Nights of Love and War* (Monthly Review Press) and, more recently, *The Book of Embraces* and *We Say No* (W. W. Norton). "The Story of the Lizard . . ." is from *Ameristories,* a work in progress, and is the first section to be published in any language.

Jorie Graham is the author of four volumes of poetry, most recently *Region of Unlikeness* (Ecco Press—the paperback will be published in July). She lives in Iowa City and teaches at the University of Iowa.

Henry Green, one of the great English-language writers of our century, was born in 1905 and died in 1973. He was the author of nine novels, several short stories, and a "mid-term autobiography." *Surviving*, a collection of Green's unpublished writings, including "Mood," will be published next year by Viking Penguin. For more on Henry Green, please see the note by Jeremy Treglown, p. 47.

Steven Hartman was born in Elmira, New York, in 1965. For the past year he has been living in Sweden, where he has a Fulbright grant to work on his second novel. His fiction has appeared in *Columbia, Folio,* and *Vox*. With the assistance of Lo Dagerman, he is currently translating a collection of Stig Dagerman's short stories, from which "To Kill a Child" is taken.

George Hixson, born in New York in 1956, lives and works in Houston as a fine art photographer and illustrator.

David Holper, originally from California, thumbed his way three times across the U.S., fought fires in Calaveras County, drove a cab in Alaska, fixed roofs in Virginia Beach, bided his time as a Russian linguist in Germany with the U.S. Army, completed an M.F.A. in fiction at UMass Amherst, and is presently surviving a stint as a high school English teacher in his home state.

Matt Jasper survived by eating nothing but communion wafers for twenty-three years. Every Friday his body would re-create the wounds of Christ. He wept blood, spoke in languages he'd never studied, and healed the terminally ill. Those wishing to contribute to his memorial fund may do so care of Post Office Box 356, Durham, New Hampshire 03824.

Sherrie Levine was born in Hazelton, Pennsylvania. A survey of her work organized by the Kunsthalle, Zürich, has also been presented at the Westfälisches Landesmuseum, Münster, and the Rooseum–Center for Contemporary Arts, Malmö, Sweden; it is currently on exhibit at the Hôtel des Arts, Paris. Levine lives and works in New York City, where she is represented by the Mary Boone Gallery.

David Mason's first book of poems, *The Buried Houses,* was co-winner of the 1991 Nicholas Roerich Poetry Prize and has been published by Story Line Press.

Friederike Mayröcker is known for the baroque quality of her poetry and "hallucinatory prose." She has received a number of prizes, including the Georg-Trakl-Prize (1977) and the Grosser Oster-reichischer Staatspreis (1982). Other translations of her work can be found in *The Vienna Group: 6 Major Austrian Poets,* translated and edited by R. Waldrop and H. Watts (Station Hill Press, 1985).

W. S. Merwin was born in New York City in 1927. His book of prose *The Lost Upland* has just been published by Knopf; a new book of poems, *Travels,* is forthcoming (also from Knopf). Merwin's other books of poetry include, most recently, *The Rain in the Trees,* as well as *The Carrier of Ladders,* for which he was awarded the Pulitzer Prize in 1970.

Sylvia Plachy's photographs appear regularly in *The Village Voice.* A collection of her work, *Unguided Tour,* recently received the Inter-national Center for Photography's Infinity Award for best photo-graphic book published in 1991. This summer she will present an audiovisual work, *The Phantom Limb,* at Les Rencontres Interna-tionales de la Photographie in Arles, France.

Peter Redgrove is widely regarded as a leading British poet. He is also a novelist, a playwright, and coauthor (with Penelope Shuttle) of *The Wise Wound,* the revolutionary study of the human fertility cycle. His latest book of poems, *Under the Reservoir,* was published this year. He lives with his wife and daughter in Cornwall, U.K.

Alastair Reid is a writer and poet who divides his time between New York and Latin America. He has translated several volumes of Pablo Neruda's poetry and is the author of *Weathering: Poems and Translations* and *Whereabouts: Notes on Being a Foreigner,* which has recently been reissued by White Pine Press.

Nancy Rexroth lives and works in Cincinnati. In the 1970s she was a pioneer in the use of the Diana, a low-cost, disposable camera manufactured in Hong Kong. *Iowa,* a book of her Diana photographs, was published in 1977.

Kathryn Rhett lives in San Francisco. Her poems have appeared in *The Antioch Review, Ploughshares,* and elsewhere.

Gerhard Richter has long been an important and influential figure in postwar European art, and his work has been featured in major exhibitions in Paris, Eindhoven (The Netherlands), Stuttgart, and Düsseldorf, among many others. A major retrospective of his work was held last year at the Tate Gallery in London. Richter lives and works in Düsseldorf.

Edward W. Said teaches literature at Columbia University. His most recent books are *Musical Elaborations* and a new, revised edition of *The Question Of Palestine.* His forthcoming book is *Culture and Imperialism,* to be published in early 1993 by Knopf. He wishes he knew Greek a little better.

Gary Snyder lives in the northern Sierra Nevada, and teaches part of the year at the University of California in Davis. His selected poems, *No Nature,* will be out this fall.

Alan Soldofsky is the author of a chapbook of poems, *Kenora Station* (Steam Press). His work has appeared in *The Antioch Review, Blue Mesa Review, The Indiana Review, Poetry East,* and other periodicals. He teaches at San Jose State University, where he directs the Center for Literary Arts.

Johan Theron was born in South Africa in 1924. His mother was Dutch, having emigrated from Holland with her family in 1914. He studied literature and law, joined the South African diplomatic service in 1947 and the United Nations Secretariat in 1957. There his senior assignments included that of Deputy Director of the Budget and, finally, Chief Editor. He retired in 1985 and lives in Manhattan.

CONTRIBUTORS

Guy Trebay's "Dunes" was published in *Grand Street* 36. His writing appears in *The Village Voice, The New Yorker,* and many other publications.

Jeremy Treglown edited the *Times Literary Supplement* from 1982 to 1990. He has written introductions to reissues of four of Henry Green's novels so far, and his life of Roald Dahl is to be published by Farrar Straus Giroux sometime in 1993. He spent the first semester of 1992 teaching at Princeton.

Rosmarie Waldrop's most recent books of poems are *The Reproduction of Profiles* (New Directions) and *Peculiar Motions* (Kelsey St. Press).

David Foster Wallace is the author of *The Broom of the System* and *Girl With Curious Hair.* His "Forever Overhead" will appear in *The Best American Short Stories: 1992.* "Three Protrusions" is excerpted from a longer work.

Lawrence Weschler has covered Poland for *The New Yorker* for over a decade. His earlier pieces were collected in *The Passion of Poland* (Pantheon, 1984). His most recent book, *A Miracle, A Universe: Settling Accounts With Torturers* (Pantheon, 1990), deals with the recent histories of Brazil and Uruguay. His art writings include a biography of Robert Irwin and *Shapinsky's Karma, Boggs's Bills, and Other True-Life Tales* (North Point, 1988).

Sebastian Yorke is fifty-eight and the only son of the English novelist Henry Green. He followed a similar education to his father and in 1959 took over the family engineering firm in Leeds, Yorkshire, which he has run ever since. He does not write novels and, having sound hearing, has no ear for dialogue like his father.

For many years the typographer **Stephen Bencze** was an esteemed member of the graphic arts community in Houston. He died in April of this year. He worked tirelessly to support the production of *Grand Street,* and he will be greatly missed.

ILLUSTRATIONS

cover & title page Sherrie Levine, *Untitled (After Duchamp: Chessboards) #4* (details), 1989. Collection of The Eli Broad Family Foundation, Santa Monica, California. Courtesy of the artist and Daniel Weinberg Gallery, Santa Monica. Photographs by Douglas M. Parker Studio.

p. 10 Mel Chin, *Rilke's Razor (Jung's Version)* (detail), 1990, straight razor, rosewood, velvet and mirror, 9¾ x 6 x 2¼ in. Collection of Carolyn Farb, Houston. Courtesy of Frumkin Adams Gallery, New York, and William Steen. Photograph by George Hixson.

p. 22 Green family photograph, c. 1910. Courtesy of Sebastian Yorke.

p. 46 Henry Green, 1923. Signed "Henry Michaels" (an early pen name). Courtesy of Sebastian Yorke.

pp. 82, 84, 86, 88, 90, 92 Sherrie Levine, *Fountain (After Duchamp: 1–6)*, 1991, bronze, 15 x 25 x 15 in. Courtesy of the artist and Mary Boone Gallery, New York. Collections:
No. 1. Doris Lockhart, London
No. 2. Marc Blondeau, Paris
No. 3. Phillipe Segalot, Paris
No. 4. Private collection
No. 5. Tom Patchett, Los Angeles
No. 6. John Sacchi, New York.

pp. 83, 85, 87, 89, 91, 93 Sherrie Levine, *La Fortune (After Man Ray: 1–6)*, 1990, felt, mahogany, and billiard balls, 33 x 110 x 60 in. Courtesy of the artist and Mary Boone Gallery, New York. Collections:
No. 1. Lannan Foundation, Los Angeles
No. 2. Museum of Contemporary Art, Los Angeles
No. 3. Walker Art Center, Minneapolis
No. 4. Whitney Museum of American Art, New York
No. 5. Pentti Kouri, Greenwich, Connecticut
No. 6. Vijak Mahdavi and Bernardo Nadal-Ginard, Boston.

p. 96 Gerhard Richter, *Scheune*, 1984, oil on canvas, 38 x 40 in. Courtesy Marian Goodman Gallery, New York.

p. 102 Mark Flood, untitled, 1989, acrylic on found painting (acrylic on canvas), 16 x 20 in. Private collection. Photograph by George Hixson.

pp. 118, 121, 123, 124, 127, 129, 131 Photographs by Sylvia Plachy.

p. 134 Nancy Rexroth, *House With Melting Roof, Pomeroy, Ohio*, 1971, silver gelatin print from Diana camera. Courtesy of the artist and Mark Power.

ILLUSTRATIONS

p. 142 Nancy Rexroth, *Folding House, New Lexington, Ohio,* 1974, silver gelatin print from Diana camera. Courtesy of the artist and Mark Power.

p. 145 Nancy Rexroth, *Waving House, Vanceburg, Kentucky,* 1975, silver gelatin print from Diana camera. Courtesy of the artist and Mark Power.

pp. 153, 157, 159 Photographs by Michele Laurent. Courtesy of Gamma Liaison.

pp. 154, 155, 156, 158 Photographs by Martine Franck. Courtesy of Magnum Photos.

pp. 161–168 Photographs by Bengt Wanselius. Courtesy of SFF Fotografirrätten.

pp. 182, 184, 185, 187, 188 Woodcuts by J. Borges.

pp. 192, 197, 202, 209, 216, 223 Six stencils (artists and titles p. 226), spray paint on paper, c. 11½ x 8 in. Courtesy of Piotr Bikont.

p. 238 Anonymous poster from lower Manhattan, November 1991.

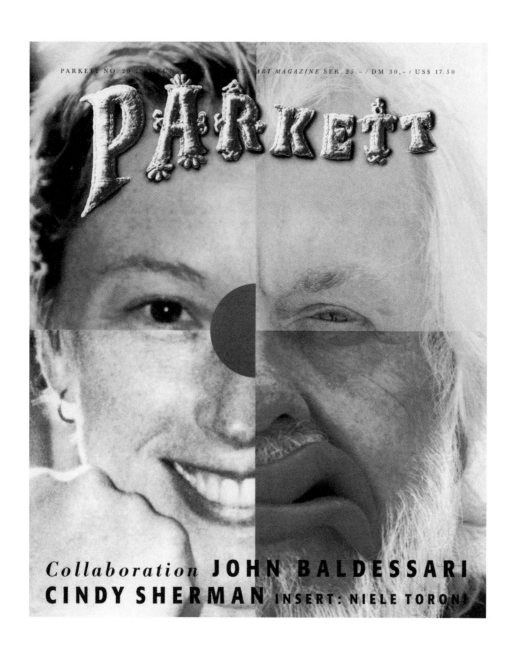

ARTHUR MILLER · LOUISE BOURGEOIS

a collaboration

Peter Blum Edition is proud to present
the previously unpublished story

Homely Girl, A Life by Arthur Miller
with accompanying images by Louise Bourgeois

Photograph by Inge Morath

This publication consists of two volumes
printed by letterpress on Mohawk Superfine
paper in cloth binding with slipcase.
Volume I contains *Homely Girl, A Life* with
ten drawings by Louise Bourgeois.
Volume II presents eight full-color, double
page collages by Louise Bourgeois with the
text by Miller.

The book is published in an edition of 1200
copies. The first 200 copies are signed by
Miller and Bourgeois.

The Deluxe Edition of 150 includes ten
etchings by Louise Bourgeois, a special
binding and slipcase.

Available from Peter Blum Edition
14 West 10th Street, New York, NY 10011 (212) 475-0227

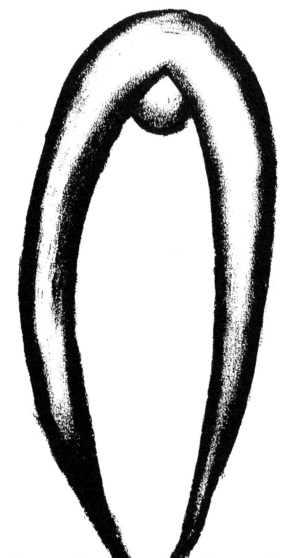

Not based on actuality; but on the wishes, dreams and aspirations of a people

Boris Vian
Translated by Julia Older
Foreword by Louis Malle

Blues for a Black Cat and Other Stories